Stories That Teach Girls

A 30-Day Walk Through

Girls' Life Lessons with God's Word

Written by:

IANTHA USSIN (Ms. I.)

Copyright ©2016 by Iantha Ussin. All rights reserved.

Stories that Teach Girls: A 30-Day Walk Through Girls' Life Lessons with God's Word. Printed in the United States of America.

No portion of this book may be reproduced, stored in a retrieval system, or transmitted in any form or by any means except for brief quotations in printed reviews without the prior written permission of Iantha Ussin.

Unless otherwise indicated, all scripture quotations are taken from the Holy Bible, New King James Version. Copyright 1982 by Thomas Nelson, Inc. Used by permission. All rights reserved.

Scripture taken from the HOLY BIBLE, NEW INTERNATIONAL VERSION. Copyright 1973, 1978, 1984 by International Bible Society. Used by permission of Zondervan. All rights reserved.

Interior/Exterior Graphic Design by Karolyne Roberts from IAMIMAGE.COM.

ISBN – 978-0-692-79082-3

TABLE OF CONTENTS

Dedication vi

Foreword viii

Introduction: I HAD TO Write This Book 11

How to Get the Most Out of This Book 15

The Price 20

A Special Design 70

The White Scarf 120

Family Ties, Part 1 174

Family Ties, Part 2 198

DAY 29: What is Quiet Time? 228

Day 30: My Quiet Time 234

DEDICATION

*This book is dedicated to every girl I've ever taught,
and every girl I will ever teach about the love God has for her through Jesus Christ.
It's dedicated to every girl I've introduced to a relationship with Jesus.
To every girl who's ever learned, or will learn from me what it looks like to be a girl who honors
God with her life—the way she talks, the way she dresses, the way she behaves, the way she
treats others—this book is for all of you.*

Foreword

Stories THAT TEACH Girls

A young black female being raised in the south requires the presence of God in her household. Early in my life, I was ensured that a God loved me and cared for me, but I was incapable of comprehending how everyone knew this. Through Ms. I's storytelling and teachings, a window of understanding opened in my young, developing mind. She simply could not settle for the typical *"God loves you. Jesus died for you. Sin is bad. Accept Jesus into your heart."* It's the intimate details she mentions like the hairs on our heads being numbered that fascinates young ladies into developing a relationship with God. Being knit together in my mother's womb and God knowing me before I knew myself is what boggled my mind. Through countless tales of sinners being spared and females realizing their worth through fighting temptations, she seamlessly connects what appears to be fiction into real life situations that every girl will soon have to endure. Standing firm in the word of God, I know that these are not mere fables. These are opportunities in which one may find a way to connect with the Lord.

I have battled a long journey of finding myself, suffering from depression, anxiety, and societal pressure but I have been taught that I have purpose, that God can love a born sinner like me, and that I am a disciple of Him. I am obliged to thank Ms. I. for her teachings and her vision to spread the Gospel. She has instilled in me scripture, understanding, and love. She is fulfilling her purpose by simply showing me I have one. I'm grateful.

Asia Lee, Age 17
Praise Movement School of Dance
Dancer, 2008 – 2015
Instructor, 2016

Foreword

If I could describe Ms. I's teaching in one word, it would be "necessary". It has been essential to me maturing into a young woman.

I walked away from dance camp every summer with a newfound love and respect for my mind and body as a temple in Jesus Christ. Her teaching makes you feel God's love for you so passionately, despite your past mistakes, that you have no choice but to love yourself again. Her unique way of teaching girls how to combine their talents and hobbies with their love for God is why I will never forget scriptures like Romans 6:13 and 1 Corinthians 6:19. I believe that the respect and approach I receive from others today is a direct result of how I've been nurtured by Ms. I's godly character and biblical wisdom. Her teaching brings out a vibrant beauty in girls from the inside out. Her teaching led me to give my life to Christ. Her teaching is why I know that I am a part of His kingdom, and why I teach girls everywhere that we are and will forever be **royalty**.

Sassett West, Age 22
Praise Movement School of Dance
Dancer, 2009-2011
Instructor, 2012-2013

Introduction:
I had to Write This Book

Introduction:
I Had To Write This Book

When the Lord gave me the vision for *Praise Movement School of Dance* (summer dance camp) in 2004, He was very clear on how the schedule for each day should look. Yes, it would be a dance camp, but it would focus, first, on teaching girls the word of God. They would learn the word of God and then learn how to "speak" His word through dance. They would take His word and dance it out so others could learn about God from "listening" to them. When the Lord gave me the very first plans for the dance camp very early one morning, I wrote the daily schedule down in my journal just the way He gave it to me.

8:00 – 8:30	Breakfast
8:30 – 9:30	**Spiritual Food**
9:30 – 10:15	Stretching and Exercise
10:15 – 10:30	BREAK
10:30 – 12:00	Dance Session 1 (Age Group)
12:00 – 12:45	Lunch
12:45 – 2:15	Dance Session 2 (Whole Group)
2:15 – 2:30	BREAK
2:30 – 3:00	Romans Road to Salvation / Eternal Life Rap / Dismissal

We would start the day with breakfast (physical food), and that would be followed by God's word (spiritual food). Before anything else would happen in the day, the girls would get God's word. And so it was. That camp and every one of the 11 camps since that first one in 2005 has followed pretty much the same schedule (the days are longer now). No girl who has come through *Praise Movement* has left without God's word planted in her heart. No girl who has come through *Praise Movement* has danced a song without understanding the message in the song. And I wouldn't have it any other way! Every day of the 6-day camp is designed to teach the word of God all day—from the prayer talk at breakfast, to the spiritual food session, to the break down of lyrics in dance sessions, to the Jesus music we jam to at lunch—it's all about HIM!

But what happens when the girls leave camp? How many of them are being fed the word of God outside of *Praise Movement*? How many of them get taught the word of God on a daily basis like they are taught at camp? It wasn't until the 2015 dance camp that those questions really bothered me. Sure, in years past, I'd thought about it. I'd even said a couple of times before that the girls needed something they could take home with them that would keep them hungry and excited about God's word. I told myself that they needed to have their daily doses of His word, and I felt responsible for making sure they got it. I remember introducing the dancers at the 2012 dance camp to a Quiet Time (*you'll learn about Quiet Time later in the book*). In their folders for that week, they were given step-by-step instructions on how to have daily Quiet Time with the Lord, but because the Spiritual Food session each day was an actual lesson to teach them the Word of God and how to apply it to their lives, I didn't have time to ***show*** them how to do a Quiet Time.

Then, in 2013, 2014, and 2015, I made it my business to not only teach the word of God in our spiritual food sessions, but I made sure I ***showed*** the girls how to do a Quiet Time too. I set aside a day where I showed them, step by step, what to do, and then on the next day, they applied what they learned. I was getting closer to teaching them how to meet with, and talk to the Lord and how to allow Him to talk to them, but that still wasn't enough for me.

What I've noticed over the years is that the girls are excited about learning God's word when they're at *Praise Movement* because they have someone

Introduction:
I Had To Write This Book

teaching it to them in a way they understand. They are excited about the Spiritual Food sessions because I tell them stories that connect to the word of God. They remember God's love and they remember Jesus' sacrifice because they can tie it to the stories they hear. And they ***always*** want more! With that realization, it finally clicked in my head. Finally, the Lord spoke to me about the desire He placed in my heart for the girls to have His word before them on a regular basis. He showed me how to give them a way to meet with Him every day so it becomes like second nature to them, and so it becomes the desire of their hearts. He told me to send them home with a book. He told me to write a book with stories that connect them to His word. He told me to write a book that allows them to write their thoughts and make connections between what they read in the stories and what they read in His word. He told me to teach them, even further, how to have Quiet Time with Him. He told me to give them something to help them draw closer to Him so He could draw closer to them. And *Stories That Teach Girls* is the result.

How to Get the Most Out of This Book

What You Need

- This Book, of course ☺

- Your Bible

Be sure to have a bible that you understand. The King James Version (KJV) is sometimes harder to understand because it is written in the language that was spoken in Bible days. This is why other versions of the bible were developed. Different versions take what God's word says and make it a bit easier to understand. I suggest the New International Version (NIV) or the New Living Translation (NLT).

- A Pen

- A Highlighter (optional)

The Book Tour

I encourage you to flip through and skim the pages of the book before you dig in and get started because you won't be just reading, you'll be writing. There are 4 stories in this book. You are expected to spend 1 week with each story, so you'll have 4 weeks with the stories (and 2 days of Quiet Time). Each story will teach you something (some things) different, and each day within each story will teach you something different. There's just a whole buRnch (my favorite "Ms. I. word") of good stuff in here for you!

With books like these, where you're expected to read and reflect, you get the most out of them when you digest a little at a time. Reading the entire book and trying to work through it all in one day is not as beneficial as taking it one day at a time. Taking small bites gives you time to meditate on what you study. To get the most out of this book with deeper understanding and a lasting impact of God's word on your heart, follow the plan for each story. I KNOW that God designed it this way for you. Trust His design and do it like He says.

Day 1 – Read the Story and Complete the Day 1 Study

Day 2 – Complete the Day 2 Study

Day 3 – Complete the Day 3 Study

Day 4 – Complete the Day 4 Proverbs Study

Day 5 – Complete the Day 5 Activity/Challenge

Day 6 – Complete the Day 6 Study

Day 7 – Complete the Journal Exercise

When to Read and Study

All of our lives are different. Our families' ways of living aren't all the same. It would be good if you start your day with your reading and study, but if your mornings are jam packed and you have to hustle and bustle to get out of the house, it's obvious that mornings won't work for you. That was the case in my parents' house when I was growing up. For me, the time I had right after school was my time. I would get home from cheerleading practice and go straight up to my room. That's where I would do my homework. That was always a relaxing time for me. I could take my time through each assignment and move at my own pace. When I think back to that time, I can see that it would've been great for me to start my homework session AFTER my time with the Lord. Unfortunately, I wasn't like you when I was in middle and high school. No one had taught me the word of God. I wasn't hungry to learn about Him at that age. But if I had been, I KNOW that would have been my time. It was the BEST time. It probably would have given me amazing insight into some of those tough assignments too.

If the morning or the after school time doesn't work for you, another great time is right before bed. I actually utilize the before bed time in my life right now. I'm always reading something before I go to bed, and if I didn't already talk to the Lord and spend time reading and journaling in the morning, I get my pillows all set up in my bed, I get my bible and journal (and book, if I'm reading one), and I get down into some time with the Lord. This time is good too because you can pray before you go to bed, sleep on it, and spend the entire next day meditating on what you studied.

You don't have to start on Sunday as your Day 1. You can start on whatever day you want, but try your very best to be consistent and not skip a day. You want to build on what you're learning, and the more time you spend with the Lord on a consistent basis, the better you hear Him. Your relationship with God builds and becomes stronger the more time you spend together. Some girls will start on Tuesday, so their Day 1 will always be Tuesday. Some girls will start on Monday, so their Day 1 will always be Monday. It doesn't matter when you start. Start when you want, but be consistent. *(I recommend starting on a day of the week when you have the most time to yourself. The Day 1 studies of each week are a bit heavier than the other days.)*

Make It Yours

I don't know about you, but I'm an active reader. I write ALL OVER my books when I read. I underline, I circle, and I write little notes to myself in the margins and at the top and bottom of the pages. I just make the book mine. When I interact with my reading, I understand it more. When I "talk back" to the book, it's more like a conversation instead of me just reading. That's why this book is a **work**book. My desire is for you to not only learn from the stories and from the word of God, but for you to talk to the Lord while He talks to you through the words on these pages. Years later, you'll be able to come back to this book and reflect on what the Lord was teaching your heart at that moment in time. You'll be able to revisit the lessons you learned if you need to remind yourself, and you can share your thoughts with others as you minister to them about what the Lord taught you. I have SEVERAL study books and workbooks from the early years of my relationship with God, and I can remember visiting those books later to remind myself when I needed reminding, to encourage myself when I needed encouraging, and to simply refresh myself when I needed refreshing. Don't just read. Interact with your reading!

Are you ready to dig in?

The Price

by Iantha Ussin (Ms. I.)
Inspired by a story heard from a friend

Stories THAT TEACH Girls

It was Christmas in a little town called Sinasia, and Christmas was big there. Every year, many of the families would get together at each other's houses to cook and sing carols and just enjoy one another's company because like most of our families, they had family members that they would only see at that one time of year. They wanted to savor every moment.

Christmas was REALLY special at one particular family's house because the adults in the Deatharus family took pride in making sure the children had everything they wanted. They would prepare for a long time—sometimes starting in July—to make sure every child had their wish. This year, though, was extremely difficult for one woman in the family. Her name was Asinna.

Usually Asinna would have it all together, but this year she had to stop working because of back, knee and kidney problems. Her conditions were so bad sometimes that she couldn't walk. She had days when she couldn't even pull herself from the bed. Most of the time, she would be in so much pain that she'd take sleeping pills and just sleep for hours so she wouldn't have to feel the pain. If the pain was still there when she woke up, she'd repeat the process—take the pills and go to sleep.

One day, about 3 days before Christmas, Asinna happened to be feeling a little better than usual. She realized that she hadn't been herself for a while because she was so depressed about not being able to do anything for her family for Christmas. She decided that this day was her day to do something. She knew she had no money, and she knew she couldn't ask family for any more money, but she still got up and got herself together to go into town. She would make a way.

Asinna walked to town and browsed through all of the shops. Her eyes lit up when she saw all of the beautiful things she could get for the children in the family. She wanted it all, but she had to decide on something small that she'd be able to give to both the boys and the girls. She had purposely put on really big clothes to hide whatever she decided to get, but she still didn't want to get anything too big and risk her chances of being caught. Asinna knew the penalty for stealing in Sinasia was chopping off of the hand and a public lashing with a whip, but she kept telling herself that she wouldn't get caught and that she just HAD TO get something special for the children for Christmas.

    She decided on some beautiful, multi-colored fabric that she would use to make each child a scarf. She would just pull out her old sewing machine and have them all done in no time. Asinna got as much as she thought she'd need and hid it in her clothes. Just as she was heading to the door to leave the shop, the cashier walked from behind the counter toward her and said, "Ma'am, you're not going anywhere. I've already called the police because I saw you stealing."

    Before Asinna could get the next step planted on the ground, a police officer came from what seemed like thin air and grabbed her by the arm.

    He said, "Ma'am, do you know the penalty for stealing in Sinasia?"

    With tears forming in her eyes and a whimper in her voice, she said, "Yes, but I just needed to get this for my family for Christmas. See, I'm sick and I have no job and no money and..."

    But the officer stopped her and said, "You know the penalty. There's no excuse. You were caught stealing."

    He grabbed hold of both of her arms and walked her to his patrol car. He saw how she limped and how she walked bent over at the waist. He could tell she was in pain. He thought to himself, *"How in the world is this woman going to be able to handle 30 lashes. They'll kill her!"* But he went on with the procedure. She cried and cried and cried, but he had to enforce the law.

When they got down to the station, the police officer explained Asinna's situation to the chief.

He said, "But Chief, I just don't know if she can handle 30 lashes AND having her hand cut off."

The chief said, "Well, she could handle stealing couldn't she? Set her lashing for Christmas Eve."

Asinna sat in jail that night and the next, and the police officer would see her and try to figure out how to save her from such a harsh punishment because of her condition. He felt awful! He talked each day with the chief to see if he could change his mind, but the chief held his ground.

Christmas Eve came, and the whole town knew that Asinna was receiving 30 lashes downtown at the City Square. Her family begged the chief to give another punishment because of her condition, but just as he did with the police officer, the chief stood his ground.

The police officer had to walk Asinna up to the platform to receive her lashings because he was the one who made the arrest. As he walked her up and all of the people were crying and shouting, the police officer said, "Wait! Stop your crying! I hear you, and I know that if this woman takes these lashes, she'll die."

He began to take off his shirt. He walked behind Asinna and stretched out his arms to cover her and said, "Chief, I will take the lashes for her."

The people sighed with disbelief. Silence fell over the crowd.

The Price

The chief looked the police officer square in the eye and said, "You really don't have to do this again."

When the police officer took off his shirt, it was evident that he had taken lashes before. He had scars and welts all over his back and shoulders.

The police officer said, "I know I don't have to, Sir, but I want to. Let me do this for her."

Stories THAT TEACH *Girls*

The Price: Day 1 Study

Sin

Read Romans 3:23. Write it below.

_____

_____

The verse says that **ALL** have sinned. ALL! EVERYBODY! Momma, daddy, favorite big cousin, auntie, pastor, choir director, that nice lady at church, you, me...**EVERYBODY!**

What, then, is **SIN**? We know what the verse says, and we know that everyone has sinned (does sin), but what is it?

Back when I was in college, I worked at a Christian sports camp in the summers. At that camp, we were responsible for sharing the word of God with children and introducing them to a relationship with Jesus Christ. One of my friends from that camp taught the children a definition for sin, and it's been with me ever since. I teach it everywhere I go. She said, ***"Sin is anything we say, think, or do that does not please God."***

Highlight (or underline) the definition of sin.

The Price

That means we've all *said* something that doesn't please God; we've all *thought* something that doesn't please God; we've all *done* something that doesn't please God. All of us. And God hates it.

What is the name of the town from the story?

_____

This means everyone there did/does what?

_____

What was the main character's name?

_____

The name of the town speaks for itself, and the main character's name tells us exactly who she is. She is **A-SIN-NA** (a sinner), and she lives in a place that is full of others who sin, which is much like the places where you and I live.

Asinna, like you and I, did something that doesn't please God. She was going through a rough time. She was suffering from all of her physical ailments. She was depressed and down on herself. The one thing that would make her feel better, she thought, was getting something special for the children in her family for Christmas. But there was one problem: she had no money. The only way she was going to get it was if she stole it, so that's what she did.

How did you know Asinna was going to steal the fabric?

Before Asinna even left her house, she had it settled in her mind that she would steal the fabric. She purposely wore oversized clothing so she could hide it. God is not pleased when we plan in our minds to do something that doesn't please Him. He's not pleased when we plan to sin.

Most people, if they read *The Price*, would say that Asinna was tempted to sin because she had no money. They would say she had to do something so she could have gifts for the children for Christmas, but God's word says that He doesn't tempt us. His word says in James 1:13-15 that **we're tempted by our own evil desires**. Our own evil desires push us and pull us and eventually cause us to end up in sin. An easy way to sum all of that up is to simply say, ***our thoughts eventually become our actions***. If you continually think on it and you don't exercise some self-control and shut those thoughts down, eventually, you'll do it. We can't say anyone or anything made us do it. *We* made us do it. *I* made me do it. *You* made you do it. *Asinna* made Asinna do it.

THE PRICE

Read Proverbs 6:16 and 6:18. Write verse 18 below.

_____

_____

The Bible says God HATES a heart that devises (plans out) wicked schemes. When we plan to sin, the Lord is not pleased.

Look at Proverbs 6 again. Read verses 16-19. From each verse, write down what the Lord hates.

Verse 17

_____

_____

Verse 18

_____

_____

Stories THAT TEACH Girls

Verse 19

_____

_____

    Haughty eyes (a proud look) - A proud look reflects a heart that's full of pride. When someone has pride in their heart, they think they're better than others; no one can tell them anything. They think way too high of themselves. If you put yourself above others like you're the best thing that ever happened to the world, that's the kind of pride the Lord hates. The pride in your heart shows up on your face (haughty eyes) and is reflected in your actions.

    A lying tongue is a lying tongue—period. If you tell a lie, it's a lie, no matter how big or how small you may think it is. The Lord hates it.

    Hands that shed innocent blood is what it means to take someone's life or intentionally cause them harm outside of self-defense.

    Feet that are quick to rush into evil - Do you run to the fights at school? Are your ears quick to find out the latest gossip? Do you jump on board with your friend when you know she's about to disobey her parents? Do you go along with her when you know she's about to go into that store in the mall and steal? Are YOU the one who's so quick to disobey your parents or anyone else in authority over you? Are YOU the one going into that store in the mall to steal? Basically, if you don't hesitate to do wrong, and you jump right into it without even having a second thought, your feet are quick to rush into evil, and the Lord hates it.

A false witness who pours out lies – Have you ever lied on someone to keep yourself out of trouble, like when you know *both* of you were there when the issue occurred, but you blamed it all on the other person? That's an example of a false witness. Or, you could have lied *for* someone to get them out of trouble. For instance, you know your friend was the one who wrote on the wall in the restroom because you saw her, but when your teacher asks you if you know who did it, you say you don't know who it was because you don't want to be a snitch. The Lord hates it. He hates when you lie to cover someone and when you lie to cover yourself. And what if you just come up with something completely false altogether, like some have been known to do with rumors? There have been instances where people created lies about someone they didn't like or because they wanted to get back at someone, and they spread those lies around. The Lord hates it.

A man who stirs up dissension among brothers – Today, we live in a social media-driven society. The biggest misunderstandings, arguments, and unnecessary fights that I've seen over the past 7 of my 11 years as a school teacher have been as a result of social media. And why? Because it's easy to sit behind a computer or a phone and say things. It's easy to be "messy" because all I have to do, for example, is post a picture of my friend's boyfriend with another girl and tag my friend in it so she can see. And just like that, I've started a war. When they get to school the next day, there WILL BE drama, and I was the cause of it. I stirred up (boosted) dissension (mess, misunderstanding, chaos) among brothers (or any people who were in good standing with each other). The Lord hates it.

And there are so many other scenarios I could place under each example of what the Lord hates, but I know that you get a clear picture of the types of things the Lord hates from what I've shared. I wanted to break these things down because sometimes, we honestly don't think we're doing anything wrong. These things, however, are things that break the Lord's heart. These things are **SIN!** If you look at the examples from Proverbs 6:16-19, you'll see that each one is something that hurts someone else somehow, even if it's just hurting their feelings.

List 3 things that you've done in the last 6 months that you know did not please God.

1. _____
2. _____
3. _____

Choose one thing from your list. On the lines below, explain how you know it wasn't pleasing to God.

_____

_____

_____

The Lord desires for us to love others and to be kind to them. He wants us to live together in harmony, not in strife and always at odds with one another. He expects us to find ways to be friendly. He wants us to run away from fights rather than run to them. He wants us to say nice things to others and about others rather than talk negatively about them behind their backs or say things directly to them that we know will hurt their feelings. Just as the word of God shows us what God hates, it also shows us how to do things that please Him. That's why it's so important for us to read and study our Bibles so we'll know what the Lord desires of us. If we know what doesn't please God, we'll know how to stay away from it. If we know what pleases Him, we'll know how to do more of it.

After reading *The Price*, and after doing today's study, what do you think the Lord is saying directly to your heart? What do you think He wants *you* to take away from today's lesson for YOU?

_____

_____

_____

_____

Stories THAT TEACH *Girls*

The Price: Day 2 Study
INTEGRITY

Dictionary.com defines **integrity** as *adherence to moral and ethical principles; soundness of moral character; honesty.* In other words, if I could make it simple for you, integrity is *doing what's right.* That's it. And if anyone has integrity, they **do what's right AT ALL TIMES, even when no one is looking.** In *The Price*, Asinna's integrity was put to the test, and she failed. And not only did she fail, but her lack of integrity almost cost her life.

Asinna is not the only one who has had a situation before her where she had the option to do right or do wrong. We have all had (and have) those situations.

Think of a time when there was an opportunity for you to do the right thing or the wrong thing, and you did the wrong thing. Explain what happened.

_____

_____

_____

Stories THAT TEACH Girls

I can think of one myself. When I was in middle school, I would play outside a good bit. Some days, all of my neighborhood friends would be outside playing, and some days, there would be no one out there. I'd be out there by myself. I am the youngest of 3 children, so I never had any trouble amusing myself. My brother and sister were 6 and 3 years older than me and didn't want their little sister tagging along in whatever it was they were doing, so I had to learn how to play alone. In our apartment complex, there was a huge parking lot where my mom would park our car. I would ride my bike in that parking lot. I would ride in the huge open spaces; I would ride in the breezeways and under the stairways of the actual apartment buildings that surrounded the parking lot; I would even ride between the cars. I remember riding between the cars one day, and I noticed an old brown and tan station wagon had its driver window almost completely down. If I wanted to reach in, open the door and get in, I could. I couldn't believe that this person had left the window down. My mom would have killed us if we had left a window down! Growing up in New Orleans where crime was high, it was necessary for us to take every measure to be safe, and having a window even cracked was a big "NO NO" in my family. So I was amazed! That day, I leaned my bike up against the car and I just peered in. It was like a whole new world. I looked at everything that was left on the back seat. I studied everything that was on the floor of the car. There was SO MUCH stuff! It's like someone was living in there! *(Another "NO NO" in my family; our car was spotless! Mama didn't play that!)* And then my eyes made contact with the front seat and the console right beneath the stereo. There was an ashtray and it was full of coins and running over! That ashtray was pretty exciting to me because we had a neighborhood candy lady, and she had snacks for days. I would visit the candy lady pretty regularly, so I would bother my mom for change all the time. At that moment, though, the last thing on my mind was asking my mom for change. I had hit a jackpot! I could get change from RIGHT THERE! The window was down and the money was in plain sight and within my reach. That day, in particular, I wanted a frozen cup from the candy lady. They were only .25, so I looked around to see if anyone was watching, and when I saw that I was out there alone, I reached into the car, grabbed a quarter right off the top of the pile, and rolled on over to the candy lady to get a frozen cup.

I wish I could say that I was satisfied with that one time, but I wasn't. I began to ride my bike in that parking lot a lot more often. I looked for that car. And whenever it was parked there, I hoped for the window to be open, and every time, it was. EVERY time! I don't even know how many times I went in there to get change out of that ashtray, but I know it became my place to get money for the candy lady. I remember getting so bold that I went beyond just sticking my hand through the window. I remember actually opening the door once or twice because the window wasn't down far enough. I would open the door, grab what I wanted, and gently close the door.

I was a thief, and I was scared EVERY time. There was always a rush of fear that surged through me when I'd be at the window of that car. I'd scan the parking lot and look at all the windows of the apartments to see if the blinds were opened or closed. I came up with a way to make it look like I was leaning my bike up against the car to fix something on the bike so I wouldn't look too suspicious. I didn't want to get caught; I knew my mom would kill me. Then, one day, when I was in that unassuming position with my bike leaned up against the car about to reach in to grab some change, a woman came walking out of her apartment toward the parking lot, and she saw me. She saw me near the car and she saw me leaned up against it, and although it may have looked like nothing to her...although it may have looked like I was just riding my bike between cars and stopped for a rest...although that's the very thing I wanted people to think...the fear in me believed otherwise! I was TERRIFIED because I KNEW I was wrong! I just knew this woman would tell my mom! I just knew it was over for me! I froze. I stood there, straddled on my bike, leaned up against the car and locking eyes with the woman as she walked to her car that was parked on the side of the parking lot that was facing me. I didn't know if she had seen me about to reach in. I didn't know if she had been watching me from her window all this time and finally ran out to catch me so she could turn me in. All of those things were running through my mind. And that fear kept me frozen until she got whatever it was she had gone to her car to get. It wasn't until she started walking back to her apartment not even paying me any mind that the tension in my body began to release. And THAT WAS IT for me!

    I had never come close to being caught, and most times never even thought about being caught, but that one time was enough. It scared me straight. I had never come close until then, and I never wanted to come close again. That fear was enough! Any time I ever thought about stealing anything after that, I always remembered the fear I felt at that moment. I didn't ever want to experience it again. I didn't like the idea of someone seeing me as a thief. I didn't like the idea that ran through my head of the woman saying, *"I caught you, and I've **been** seeing you, and we're going right up these stairs to tell your mom."* The thought of having to confess and tell my mom that I'd been going into someone's car, someone I didn't know, was too much, and even if I *did* know, I was going into someone's car who didn't invite me in, taking something that didn't belong to me. And I did it several times! I couldn't handle it. Stealing was over for me!

I had opportunities after that. I could've taken from that same car. The windows were always opened. I've been with friends when they've stolen things. I've wanted to take little small things after that incident, but I couldn't. I learned what integrity was from that moment. I know what's right. I wouldn't do this if someone was watching, so why would I do it if I think no one's watching? I learned later in life that someone *IS* always watching. GOD is *always* watching, and He knows.

How did Asinna lack integrity in the story? Did she know what she should or shouldn't do?

_____

_____

_____

It's NEVER okay to steal, no matter what the circumstances are. If it doesn't belong to you, it's not yours. If it's for sale, it's for sale. Period. It has to be purchased in order for it to become yours.

Read James 4:17. Write it below.

_____

Stories THAT TEACH Girls

God is always watching, and He expects us to have integrity. There are things that we know we shouldn't do, and if we choose to do those things anyway, we sin.

Read Proverbs 5:21 and Proverbs 15:3. Summarize them below.

_____

_____

The Big Picture:
DO WHAT YOU KNOW YOU SHOULD DO.
DON'T DO WHAT YOU KNOW YOU SHOULDN'T DO.

Is there an area in your life where you lack integrity? Now that you know the Lord is always watching, is there anything specific in your life that you believe the Lord is pressing on your heart to stop doing because you know it doesn't please Him? Is there something that you're not doing that you need to start doing? Talk about it on the next page.

The Price

Stories THAT TEACH Girls

The Price: Day 3 Study
PRESSURE

Have you ever experienced pressure? Has anyone ever tried to get you to do something that you didn't want to do, or something that you knew was wrong to do? (CIRCLE ONE)

YES   NO

Most people know what pressure feels like and have experienced being pushed or strongly encouraged to do something that they weren't comfortable with.

Share an example of a time you experienced pressure from someone to do something, say something, or go somewhere you weren't comfortable with.

_____

_____

_____

It's unfortunate that we sometimes experience pressure from friends, family members, and others in our lives, but sometimes we bring pressure on ourselves. Isn't that crazy? We definitely do, though. Or at least I know I do. Sometimes we have it fixed in our minds that we have to do a certain thing or be a certain way because *we think* that's what others expect, or *we think* it will make us better, or *we think, we think,* **WE** *think...*

Take Tiana, for example. In middle school, everyone knew her. She was Miss Popular. She was a cheerleader. She ran track. She was vice president of the student council. She was a top student who served as a peer tutor and mentor to incoming 6th graders. Her name was always being called during school announcements for some award she'd won or for being Student of the Month or something else along those lines. But it wasn't like that freshman year at her new high school. Tiana had a good group of friends, but she still felt like she was invisible. No one outside of her group of friends ever even spoke to her, and that wasn't what she was used to. She felt invisible her entire freshman year, and it was beginning to look like it would be that way her sophomore year too.

Over time, Tiana noticed that a lot of the junior and senior girls and even some of the other sophomore girls talked to EVERYONE at school. EVERYBODY knew them! They must had gotten popular from the way they dressed, Tiana thought, because when they walked through the halls, whoever wasn't walking with them would literally stop and watch them walk from point A to point B. Tiana even had to admit that their clothes were always on point. Their outfits made a statement, and it was almost like people wanted to talk to them and be around them simply because they looked good. Tiana wanted that. She wanted to make people stop in their tracks like those girls did. She wanted to make a statement again like she had done all through middle school. She began to *think* that changing her style would be the way to get people to at least speak to her. She began to *think* that her clothes would make her popular. She began to *think* that looking a certain way was what she needed for people to "see" her. So she changed the way she dressed. And not all of a sudden, but a couple outfits here, and a couple outfits there. Her dresses got a little tighter. Her skirts got a little shorter. Her clothes, in general, were more revealing and edgy. She wouldn't have worn clothes like that ordinarily, but she began to *think* that stepping out of her comfort zone was the risk she needed to take for people to "see" her. And people noticed, just like she had hoped. In particular, the popular girls noticed. Some would tell her that her outfits were cute, but most of them would laugh. They would say things like, *"Who dressed you today?"* and *"Did you lose your other clothes? You need to go and find 'em, girl!"*

And the boys gave her the attention she was looking for too. All of a sudden, they were interested in her when they never even noticed her before. She was showing a whole lot more skin, so of course she caught their eyes. Boys would walk past her and slap her on her butt. One day when she wore a skin tight dress, a boy stopped in the middle of the crowded main hallway to watch her walk by. There was a lot of noise as students were changing classes, but it seemed like the noise came to a complete stop as the boy said loudly, *"Oooooo weeee! Just like I like my girls! NAKED! I see it all, baby girl! You need to wear that dress EVERY day!"*

Tiana was so embarrassed. She was hurt. She was getting attention, but it was the attention that she DID NOT want. And she didn't know it, but the boy in her 1st period class who liked her, Devaughn, had been building up the courage to ask for her phone number so he could ask her out on a date. When she started dressing the way she had been dressing, he backed off of that idea. Devaughn didn't like girls who dressed that way. His dad had told him that when girls wear clothes like that, they have no respect for themselves. Devaughn wanted to be with a girl who dressed respectably. Cute and trendy, but respectable.

Tiana put unnecessary pressure on herself. No one told her she needed to change the way she dressed. None of the girls she was watching told her that they got popular because of the way they dressed. Tiana just assumed they did. Tiana didn't even know them. She didn't know if they were popular because of their personalities or their grades or what. She had no clue! And she suffered as a result of it. She suffered from unnecessary, self-inflicted pressure.

Think back to this week's story, *The Price*. Asinna was very much like Tiana. Asinna's situation was different, but she put herself under some unnecessary pressure too. How did Asinna bring pressure on herself? What did *she think* she had to do?

_____

_____

_____

Asinna's family knew her situation. They knew she wasn't working. They knew she had injuries and other conditions that made it hard for her to even move some days. So why didn't Asinna think her family would understand? Sure, buying gifts for the children was the family tradition, but she wouldn't have been kicked out of the family because she COULDN'T buy gifts. No one said she HAD TO buy gifts, but *Asinna thought* she had to. She felt obligated to participate because it was the family's tradition for years, and she didn't want to gather with her family and possibly be the only one without gifts for the children. Oh, the pressure! Asinna allowed her own thinking to put her under unnecessary pressure and it ended badly for her, just like it did with Tiana. *(Caving into pressure—outside pressure **and** self-inflicted pressure—usually ends badly.)*

Can you think of a time when you put yourself under unnecessary pressure? Explain.

_____

_____

_____

_____

_____

God desires for us to live free of those kinds of pressures. He wants us to live free of cares so we can just be who He created us to be, and do what He created us to do. He doesn't want us to carry the weight of trying to do something He didn't purpose for us to do, or trying to be someone He didn't create us to be.

Read I Peter 5:7. Write it on the next page.

The Price

_____

_____

_____

If you feel like you're not popular or like no one "sees" you, pray and talk to the Lord instead of changing who you are. If you feel like you need a certain pair of shoes or certain clothes to stand out (or fit in), and it's making you want to do something outside of your character, talk to the Lord. Cast those cares onto Him. I Peter 5:7 tells us that we should cast **ALL** of our cares on the Lord *because He cares for us*. The Lord knows that we sometimes feel pressure to be different or look different or have something that we don't have, and He cares that those things concern us. He cares when things weigh on our hearts. And although He already knows when things bother us because He knows all there is to know about us, He still wants us to talk to Him about them. He wants us to share our concerns with Him; He wants to hear from us. *(This is how we develop our relationship with the Lord.)* He wants us to unload every detail of our problems and the issues of our hearts into His hands, and like a good Father, he carries them so we don't have to. ***Because He cares for us***, He WANTS to carry our load. No concern is too big or too small. He can handle them all.

Read Philippians 4:6-7.

Verse 6 (NIV) says, "Do not be anxious about _____, but in everything, by prayer and petition, with _____, present your requests to _____."

This is just another way of saying, *Don't let the cares of this world trouble your heart.* When you have a concern or a request or a desire, pray and submit your concern to the Lord and thank Him that He's taking care of it for you so you don't have to carry it anymore.

Then, **verse 7 (NIV)** says, "And the _____ of God, which transcends all understanding, will guard your _____ and your _____ in Christ Jesus."

When we have worries and concerns, our minds are not at peace. Usually, when we have things on our minds, or when our hearts are heavy with cares, those things even show up in our dreams! It becomes all consuming. But verse 7 says that when we cast our cares on the Lord, His peace will guard our hearts and minds. Every time I read that verse, I get a picture in my mind. I think of my bedroom door being closed while I'm in my bed asleep. There are 2 guards standing outside of my door on either side to make sure nothing comes in to attack me or interrupt my peaceful sleep.

Anytime anything comes near my bedroom to disturb me, the guards send them away, even if they have to use force. I'm not concerned AT ALL about anything bothering me because I know the guards will take care of it. I sleep soundly. And that's how God is when we give Him our cares. Because we cast our cares onto Him, He stands guard at the door of our minds and at the door of our hearts to keep those concerns from bothering us and disturbing the peace He gave us when we prayed.

Now, it doesn't mean that those cares and concerns won't try to "come in" and bother you throughout your days, especially if you have reminders around, but you have to remind your cares that God is standing guard at your mind and at your heart so THEY CANNOT COME IN! Remind those cares that you have given them to God and that He has them in His hands now; they're not your concerns anymore because you gave them away. If your concerns keep coming to bother you, tell them to go and bother God because He's taking care of them now! *(This also builds your relationship with God. It shows Him that you trust Him to take care of you. When relationships have trust, they get stronger and stronger.)*

If Tiana would have prayed and given her concern for popularity over to the Lord, who knows if He would have made her more popular in high school than she was in middle school? He definitely wouldn't have embarrassed her because He wants the best for her. He wouldn't have made her do something she was uncomfortable with, and he certainly wouldn't have had her to step outside of who He created her to be. She could have avoided some pain if she would have taken her concerns to the Lord and let Him guard her heart and mind with His peace. Now she may have ruined her reputation. She may be negatively popular now. People may not ever see her for who she really is because she presented someone that she wasn't, and *that's* the Tiana that was in the limelight. *That's* the Tiana that everyone knows.

The same is true for Asinna. Asinna is known around town in a way that she probably didn't want to be known. She's known as a thief, and it didn't have to be that way. Asinna could have enjoyed Christmas with her family without gifts. They could have reassured her that they understood her condition and that they knew she wasn't able to get gifts. She could have given that care over to the Lord, and who knows how He may have fixed it. He could have had another member of the family give her some gifts to give to the children. They could have given her money to buy gifts. Who knows? She ruined it because of the unnecessary pressure she placed on herself. She was too anxious to do it her own way.

Remember This: <u>**We should only change as God wants us to change**</u>. For instance, if I'm someone who's always bad mouthing people, the Lord is not pleased with that. He clearly states in His word (Ephesians 4:29) that I shouldn't let unwholesome talk come out of my mouth. I should only say things that will build others up. When I give my life to the Lord and start to live for Him, he shows me how to change my speech so it will glorify Him. He teaches me, through His word, how to have speech that encourages people and lifts them up, so I change. And that's the kind of change he wants. He doesn't want me to change in the opposite direction and go against His ways *(i.e., becoming a thief, dressing inappropriately, lying, etc.)*. If I do that, it doesn't please Him because then I'm not being who He created or **RE**created me to be. In those times, it usually ends badly.

The Price

Side Note: Christmas is a holiday that society created. It's not a holiday that God tells us in His word to celebrate. When society created Christmas, the Christian community decided to make it a day that focuses on the birth of Christ rather than focusing on the fairytale of Santa Clause and a gift-filled sleigh. Gifts are not required at Christmas; they're a choice. We don't have to feel pressured into buying gifts. If it's something you want to do, that's GREAT! You shouldn't beat yourself up if you can't afford to though. God doesn't want you under that kind of pressure. Wearing red and green is not required. Putting up a Christmas tree is not required. Decorating the house is not required. These are all things that have gained popularity over time. If you don't participate, God doesn't love you any more or any less. If you do participate, He doesn't love you any more or any less. Don't feel pressured, and don't pressure yourself. The same goes for any other thing that is outside of God's word. We shouldn't allow people to pressure us, but even more than that, we shouldn't pressure ourselves. That's not God's desire for us.

I want to leave you with one final thought. Jonathan McReynolds released a song in 2015 entitled *Pressure*. In the song, he sings...

> *I really need to rid myself*
> *Of the pressure, pressure, pressure*
> *To be someone else*
> *That the world has made.*
>
> *Jesus, take from me*
> *All the pressure, pressure, pressure*
> *To be someone that*

You did not create.
Help me
Be me
And only
See You.
Let me
Decrease
And glori-fy You.

Rid yourself of the pressure to be someone that God did not create. Focus on being who He made you and on doing what He tells you *(that's what it means to glorify Him)*. Cast ALL of your cares and concerns on Him in prayer and thank Him for giving you His peace to guard your heart and mind.

Are there any pressures or concerns that you know you need to give over to God? Write them below. After you write them, pray and give them to God. Ask Him to carry them for you.

_____

_____

_____

The Price

Stories THAT TEACH *Girls*

The Proverbs Study

On Day 4 of each week, we will do a Proverbs Study. The book of Proverbs is known as the book of wisdom because **proverb** means **a wise saying**, and because Solomon, the wisest man to ever live, wrote the book. Proverbs is FULL of wise sayings in EVERY scripture! As we're studying God's word together and learning how He wants us to live, we want to not only get knowledge of His word, but we want to gain wisdom.

Knowledge is nothing more than knowing something. **Wisdom** is when you know something and you use it, or apply it. For instance, I could know that I should eat right in order to be healthy, but if I don't use that knowledge and apply it in my own life, I'm not wise. Wisdom means I would take what I know and use it; I would eat right so I could be healthy. A wise person applies the knowledge they receive.

The book of Proverbs (one of my favorite books of the bible) is very practical because these are things Solomon learned throughout his life. It gets right down to the nitty gritty and tells it like it is! His victories and his failures and mistakes all gave him the wisdom that is included in this book. Day 4 of each week will be a day for us to look at the "straight to the point" scriptures that God used Solomon to write so we can hide them in our hearts and apply them to our lives.

The Price: Day 4

PROVERBS STUDY

Read Proverbs 2:7 and Proverbs 10:9. Write them in the boxes below.

PROVERBS 2:7	PROVERBS 10:9

Think about our topics from Days 1-3: *Sin*, *Integrity*, and *Pressure*. In the space below, summarize how today's two proverbs relate to what we've studied the past 3 days. Refer back to the studies if you need to.

Stories THAT TEACH Girls

The Challenge / Activity

On Day 5 of each week, we will have a challenge and/or an activity. The challenge will either require us to interact with others to share what we've learned in some way, or it will require us to dig deeper into our own lives and our own learning. We don't want to just know God's word for ourselves, but we want to share it with others so they can learn and grow too.

The activity will help us dig deeper into God's word so we can apply it to our lives. Sometimes, the best way to learn is to do, so to enhance our learning, we will put our hands to work.

The Price: Day 5
THE CHALLENGE / ACTIVITY

The Walking Word

The purpose of this activity is for you to memorize scripture and hide God's word in your heart. **Read Psalm 119:9-11.**

For today's activity you will need:
- Construction paper OR index cards (or another craft paper that you like to use)
- Markers OR colored pencils
- Your Bible
- Your *Stories That Teach Girls* book

Instructions
1. Look at this week's Day 1 Study. Choose one scripture from the study that stood out to you. Write it on an index card. *(If you're using construction paper or another craft paper, just fold your paper into even squares and cut them out to make cards.)* **See examples on pg. 58**
2. Jazz the card up! Make it colorful and artsy (to the best of your ability).
3. Be sure to include the actual scripture AND the address. For example, if I wrote *"Jesus wept."* on my card, I would be sure to include the address, *"John 11:35"* underneath the scripture. **See examples on pg. 58**

4. Next, look at this week's Day 2 Study, Day 3 Study, and the Day 4 Proverbs Study and choose one scripture from each study that stands out to you. Write each verse on a separate card. You should have 4 cards when you're done.
5. These cards will now become the *Walking Word*; they will "walk" around your home. Place the cards somewhere in your home where you spend a lot of time. You can put one on the mirror in your bedroom (this was my key place), one on the mirror in the bathroom, one at your desk, one on the door of the refrigerator, or any other place you can think of where you will see them every day. *(Be sure to get your parents' approval before placing the cards anywhere outside of your personal space at home.)*

You will see the scriptures daily, read them aloud and practice saying them. As you're practicing, you'll begin committing them to memory and hiding them in your heart, and before you know it, **YOU** will be the *Walking Word*. Take the cards down as you have the scriptures memorized. Put your cards in a safe place after you've memorized them all just in case you need to refresh yourself some time later. You can maybe use them as book marks for other books that you read.

Want to learn more scripture? Do this for any scripture you want to learn. It doesn't have to be for just this activity. When you live for God, there can never be too much of His word in your heart. When it's memorized and becomes a part of you, you can pull it up whenever you need it to apply it to whatever situation you face. There is power in being the *Walking Word*!

Flip the page to see the example...

Examples Of Cards for Day 5 Activity

Index Card

Using construction paper or other art paper

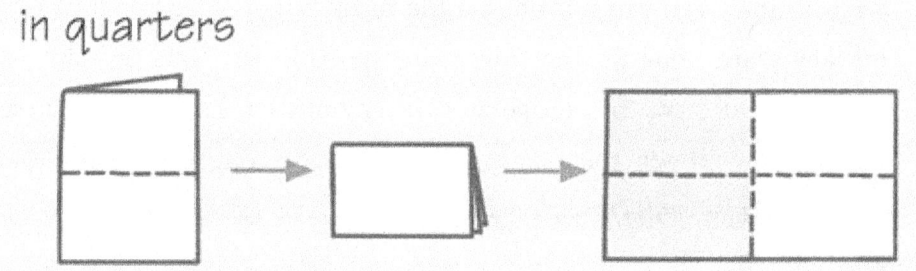

Scripture with Address

> **A gentle answer turns away wrath, but a harsh word stirs up anger.**
>
> **-Proverbs 15:1**

Stories THAT TEACH Girls

The Price: Day 6 Study

LOVE AND FORGIVENESS

Earlier this week, we talked about what sin is. We looked at some examples of things that do not please God. Keep those things in mind because today we're going to talk about how God handles our sin.

Read Romans 6:23. Write it below.

_____

_____

Let's deal with the first part of that verse that says, *"For the wages of sin is death."* **Wages** is money that is paid or received for work or services. For example, if I get paid $5 an hour and I work 40 hours a week, my wages will equal $200. It is what's owed to me for the work I did. In Romans 6:23, the Lord says that the wages of our sin is death. YES, DEATH! If you sin, your payment is death. It is what's owed to you for the sin you committed.

What was Asinna's wages for stealing the fabric?

_____

Yes, the Lord says that the wages of sin is death, but do you see people dying every time they sin? I don't. Did you die when you sinned? You obviously didn't because you're reading this book.

Now, let's be clear: **God hates sin**, and even though we don't die a physical death when we sin, the sin ***does*** cause separation between God and us, and that's what the scripture means by death. It's like saying we might as well be dead if we're separated from God, the one who created us and gave us life in the first place. It's like saying, if you're separated from Him, what life are you living anyway? There's no life in being separated from God.

Take a look at the second part of the verse. It says, *"but the gift of God is eternal life through Christ Jesus our Lord."* **But** is a conjunction that lets readers or listeners know that what comes after the ***but*** will be the opposite of what came before it. So, yes, the wages of sin is death. I *should be* dead (eternally separated from God) because of my sin, ***BUT*** the gift of God gives me life. God hates our sin, ***BUT He loves us SO MUCH that He wants to be able to look past our sin so we can be in relationship with Him.*** This is why He created a way to cover our sin, and that way is Jesus Christ. Jesus is our gift from God.

A **gift** is something that we get from others not because we deserve it, necessarily, but simply because they want us to have it. A gift says *"I'm thinking of you"* or *"You're special to me"* or *"I saw this and thought you'd like it"*. No one goes out and gets a gift because it's required; they get a gift because they want to. God gave us our gift, Jesus, to free us from the wages of sin because He loves us.

Now let's switch gears for just a second. Have you ever heard of a superstition? You know, one of those sayings like, *"If you step on a crack, you break your mama's back"* or *"If your hand is itching, you're about to get money"*?

Stories THAT TEACH Girls

Superstitions like breaking a mirror and receiving 7 years of bad luck are so real to some people. They take it to heart! Some believe that if they "split the pole", they'll have bad luck. It becomes so real to them that it becomes almost like a law that they keep. They're extra careful with mirrors and they charge everyone around them to be extra careful too. And when they're walking along a sidewalk or somewhere with someone where there's a pole, you might hear them yell, *"Don't split the pole."* It's like law to them. They're afraid that something bad is going to happen, so they take these superstitions on as rules to live by.

This is exactly how the people were in Jesus' time. When someone sinned, they would get a clean, unblemished animal (they used specific animals) and sacrifice the animal to get its blood. They would offer the blood of that unblemished animal to God in prayer and ask Him to **forgive** them. Because blood is our life source, the people used the blood as a symbol to bring life back into their lives since their sin had caused them death (separation from God). This, they believed, was what washed away their sin. Offering blood was their practice, but it wasn't a superstition. This was THE WAY of their time. It was their law, and EVERYONE had better abide by that law! There were consequences in place if someone did not offer sacrifices for their sin like they should.

Can you imagine every time you sin, having to sacrifice an animal and offer its blood to God? Can you imagine how tiring that would be? I mean, think about your own life. How many times would you have to sacrifice an animal in a day for simply rolling your eyes at someone? How many times would you have to sacrifice an animal for being disobedient or being intentionally mean or rude? It's ridiculous, isn't it? God thought so too! There was no way an animal's blood could wash away sin or forgive people's sin.

The system that the people created was a bit much. It was clear after some time that no one was going to be able to keep every little law and every little rule that they had in place. It was impossible! *(There were some RIDICULOUS laws, girl!)* They would get it right in one area, but they'd mess it up in another, and it was crazy to keep doing what they were doing to have their sins "forgiven". God could see the people's hearts though. He could see that, for the most part, they had a genuine desire to be free from sin so they could be connected to Him. God wanted to give the people something they would understand, so since they believed blood was the cleanser, and that blood was the way to get them in right standing with Him, He decided to offer ONE blood sacrifice, once and for all. There would be no more sacrificing animals over and over. There would be ONE sacrifice, and the blood from that sacrifice would have to be pure and holy and set apart because it would have to symbolize TRUE cleansing of one's sins. The only holy one was God himself, so He decided to offer His own blood to cleanse and forgive us. He took His spirit and placed it in the womb of a young woman named Mary so she could birth a child. This child was God's spirit, so he was 100% God **AND** 100% human. The child was named Jesus, and He would be THE sacrifice.

Throughout his life, even as a child, Jesus showed that He was God in so many ways. He lived a blameless life—one without sin. He performed miracles like healing sick people who had no cure for their diseases, raising people from the dead, and causing blind people to see.

Read about one of Jesus' miracles in John 9:1-12.

Jesus not only performed miracles, but wherever He would go, He would teach people how much God, His Father, loved them. He would teach them how to live in peace with one another and how to love one another. What He shared most, though, because it was God's sole purpose for creating Him and sending Him to the earth was: *My teaching is not my own. It comes from him who sent me (John 7:16). I am not here on my own, but he who sent me is true (John 7:28). The miracles I do in my Father's name speak for me (John10:2). I and the Father are one (John 10:30). He who believes in me will live, even though he dies; and whoever lives and believes in me will never die (John 11:25-26). For God so loved the world that he gave his one and only son, that whoever believes in him shall not perish but have eternal life (John 3:16). I am the way, the truth and the life. No one comes to the Father except through me (John 14:6).*

Jesus Christ (the Holy One) reminded the people over and over that He was God because He and His father, God, were one. He reminded them that if they were going to be forgiven of their sins, they had to believe that He was the only way.

They had to believe that God loved them enough to send and sacrifice His own son so they could be saved from death in sin, to life with Him. Many believed and became followers of Jesus (Christians), but there were many who didn't believe. Those who didn't believe called Jesus a liar. They were angry that He called himself God and claimed to be the only one who could save them from their sin. They still believed that they could follow the law and sacrifice animals to be saved from the death of sin. They were angry that Jesus claimed to be the King when their king, Caesar, was king. For that, they accused him of blasphemy. (**Blasphemy** *is the crime of claiming to be God or assuming to oneself the rights or qualities of God.)* Jesus was accused of breaking the law because He performed miracles on the Sabbath when no one was supposed to work. He was not received well by the officials and the leaders of that time, so they decided to crucify Him, which was common practice for those who broke the law.

Jesus knew that He had completed His work on earth, so He prepared Himself to die. He always knew that He would have to give His life for us. He knew that His whole purpose for being created was to be the ONE sacrifice whose blood would save us from death in sin to life with God. He said, *"I came from the Father and entered the world; now I am going back to the Father." (John 16:28)*

The people crucified Him on a cross, He shed His blood, hung His head, and He died. After being buried in a tomb, a few days later, the tomb was empty because He got up and ascended into heaven to sit at the right hand of God.

Jesus gave His life to cover our sin so we wouldn't have to give our own lives, and so we wouldn't have to sacrifice animals. He stood in our place as the ONE sacrifice (God himself) that would truly cleanse us and connect us to the Father.

Now think back to the story. The police officer was a lot like Jesus. Explain how the police officer was like Jesus. What did he do and what did he say that resembles what Jesus did and what Jesus said?

_____

_____

_____

Stories THAT TEACH Girls

When the police officer arrested Asinna for her crime, he knew that she should receive a public lashing and that she should have her hand cut off, but he didn't let her go through with it. Instead, he did what Jesus did for us. Rather than allowing us to receive the penalty for our crime, or the wages for our sin, Jesus took the penalty upon himself. The police officer saved Asinna from her punishment which, in her case, would have resulted in death. Jesus saves us from our punishment of spiritual death and separation from God. Asinna got to live her life even after she messed up. Those of us who are saved and covered by Jesus' blood get to live life after we mess up too. Because we accept His sacrifice as the only way to the Father, we get to have eternal life with the Father (sin can no longer separate us from God because it's covered by Jesus' blood).

Even though the story doesn't tell us, there is no doubt that Asinna was grateful to the police officer for saving her from death. Who wouldn't be? I can imagine that she felt pretty bad about having someone take her punishment for her, especially a punishment like that. In my mind, I imagine her thanking the police officer over and over. I see her visiting him for the next few weeks after that public lashing to help tend to his wounds and scars. I see her bringing him meals while he heals and doing whatever is in her power to do to make him comfortable. I imagine that she would NEVER do anything like that again because she sees the pain it caused the police officer and she never wants to cause anyone that kind of pain again. She never wants to make anyone suffer because of something she did. She always honors the police officer, from that day forward, because he sacrificed his own life so she could have hers. She feels that she owes him the ultimate respect for thinking of her in that way. Since he gave himself for her, she feels it's only right to give her life for him. She wouldn't have it any other way.

And this is why we honor Jesus. We know that we are born sinners. We know that we DID mess up, we DO mess up and we WILL mess us, and we understand that Jesus died for ALL OF THAT...sins we haven't even committed yet! How can I NOT honor the one who took the penalty for MY sin upon himself? How can I NOT give Him my life in return for Him giving His for me? All He wants for my life is for me to love others like He did when He walked the earth. He wants me to teach others about Him and tell them that His sacrifice was for them too. He wants me to tell them that they can be saved from their sin and be connected to the God who created them. His sacrifice was the ultimate example of love, and it was the ultimate example of forgiveness, and I show my ultimate appreciation for that love and forgiveness by pointing others to it so they can receive it like I did.

I'm SO grateful He gave His life for me!
For US!

The Price: Day 7

JOURNAL

Write God a letter. In the letter, tell Him everything that's stirring in your heart and mind after this week's study. Tell Him if anything has changed within you. Tell Him if this study challenged you. Tell Him how the lessons made you feel. Tell Him if the lessons compelled you to make changes in your behavior.

_____

_____

_____

_____

_____

_____

_____

The Price

_____

_____

_____

_____

_____

Have you been saved from eternal separation from God by accepting Jesus Christ and His sacrifice in your heart already?

YES   NO

If you haven't, do you want to be saved from eternal separation from God by accepting Jesus Christ and His sacrifice in your heart today?

YES   NO

If you want to be saved by accepting Jesus Christ and His sacrifice in your heart today, pray the following prayer:

Stories THAT TEACH Girls

God, I know that I'm a born sinner. I know that the wages of my sin is death and that I should be eternally separated from you, but I know you love me too much for that. I know you sent Jesus to die so His sacrifice could be the ONLY sacrifice to cover my sin. Thank you for loving me that much. Your word says, in Romans 10:9-10, "That if you confess with your mouth, 'Jesus is Lord,' and believe in your heart that God raised him from the dead, you will be saved. For it is with your heart that you believe and are justified, and it is with your mouth that you confess and are saved." And so I confess that Jesus is Lord. I believe that He died and that you raised Him from the dead. I believe that He is the only way for me to be forgiven, so I accept Jesus Christ and His sacrifice on the cross, and I ask that His spirit (your Holy Spirit) live in my heart. I thank you for saving me, Lord. Thank you for covering my sin. Thank you for loving me and forgiving me. Thank you that I AM NOW SAVED, in Jesus' name!

If you prayed that prayer, I want to welcome you to the family of believers! You are now a Christian, and now it's time for you to learn how to live like one. This book is a good start! If you don't have a church home, find one and get involved. Let the leaders know that you have accepted Jesus Christ and his sacrifice in your heart and that you're ready to grow and serve him with your life!

A Special Design
by Iantha Ussin (Ms. I.)

Stories THAT TEACH Girls

From as far back as she could remember, Kimbrel always talked about being a doctor. She and her dad would go on and on for hours about how she would one day wear her white coat, and how she would have a pink stethoscope around her neck instead of a regular black one because she would want all of her patients to know that pink is her favorite color. And if she decided to be a pediatrician, she thought a pink stethoscope would help make the doctor's visits a little less scary for the children. She could see scenarios playing out in her mind every time she and her dad talked about hospitals and needles and broken bones and ambulances—their everyday topics. Although Kimbrel loved those conversations with her dad and watching medical shows on television and learning all she could about entering into the medical field, she had a much deeper passion. Kimbrel had a passion for fashion. She absolutely LOVED clothes!

Since Kimbrel was exceptionally bright and excelled at EVERYTHING in school, she thought that she should certainly become a doctor. She thought that being anything else would be a waste of her exceptionalities. She would always hear her dad in the back of her mind saying, *"People who are naturally brilliant like you are supposed to be doctors and scientists and engineers. Everybody's not born with brains. The ones who have the brains have to make sure they put them to good use."* Kimbrel didn't want to let her dad down. She knew if she gave too much attention to her love for fashion, her dad would say she was wasting her time and wasting her excellence, and she didn't want to be a waste. She still spent time designing, of course, because it was the one thing that truly made her happy, but she continued to walk the path toward becoming a doctor because she knew she had to do more.

After high school, Kimbrel breezed through her 4 years in college and graduated with honors. Her dad beamed with great joy! His baby girl was on her way to medical school to become a doctor. Kimbrel had worked so hard and made such a name for herself in college that she became known as one of the most promising future physicians to start medical school that year. The only problem, though, was that she wasn't as excited as everyone else was about her going to medical school. She wasn't beaming with joy like her dad. She didn't care as much as everyone else did about all of the honors she'd received. And although she thought it a blessing to be considered one of the most promising future physicians of that year, she could really do without that title. She was simply going through the motions: after high school graduation, go to college; after college graduation, go to medical school; after medical school, work as a doctor. Make dad proud, even if it means the one thing that brings me true joy is put to the side.

Kimbrel's first year in medical school was just like every year of her education had been. She knew what she needed to do, so she did it. She went to class every day. She studied around the clock to make sure she aced every exam and to ensure she was prepared for every lab. She attended seminars and lectures from guest doctors that visited the school. She volunteered extra hours in the emergency room at the hospital so she could become familiar with the way things worked there. She even made time to read extra articles and books written by doctors who had been in the profession for over 15 years. Kimbrel was a pro at doing what she needed to do to "make the grade", but even while making the grade and being at the top of her class, she was miserable. The googly-eyed wonder she had as a child for ambulances, needles, broken bones and anything else related to the medical field was gone. After about 3 months into her second year in medical school, she couldn't stand to even hear the word doctor. Sitting in class became a chore, and she refused to do anything extra outside of the basic class assignments and other class-related requirements from her professors. She was spending every spare moment she had in her sewing room, designing and creating clothes. Her sketch pad and her sewing machine were her escape from it all.

Kimbrel had been designing most of her casual everyday clothes since her junior year in high school, but while in medical school, she took it up a notch. Not only did she make her casual clothes, but she made all of the outfits she wore for special occasions like the seminars she went to her first year, graduations, weddings, dinner parties and business meetings. Her friends loved everything she made. She was even asked a few times to make things for other people, and she did. They kept asking her, *"Why aren't you going into business? This is what you love, and Lord knows you're good at it."* They all saw how she'd begun spending less time in the emergency room at the hospital. They saw how she showed up to class and completed assignments and labs with little to no enthusiasm. She once participated in study groups with her friends and went to student gatherings on the weekends to relax, but that was no more. All of her friends could see that she was physically there in school with them, but they could also see that her heart was in a totally different place.

One Friday afternoon, Kimbrel's professor, Dr. Shehan, dismissed class early. The students had worked hard all week, so Dr. Shehan rewarded them with a few extra hours to enjoy the weekend. Kimbrel was sitting next to Samyra, the friend she'd had since their very first class together as medical students. Samyra was the one person who knew Kimbrel through and through, and she was the one person who knew, for sure, that medical school was never really an exciting thing for Kimbrel. Even though Kimbrel was a star student that first year, giving extra time in the emergency room and to other school related activities, Samyra saw right through it. She didn't have the passion that Samyra and all the other students had. She would ace every assignment and could go toe to toe with anyone about anything pertaining to the human body, but there was nothing in her that wanted to spend the rest of her life saving other people's lives. It just wasn't in her.

"So since this week has been one of the hardest weeks you've had this year, and because you all handled it like I expect promising future physicians to do, I am dismissing you early. We're done for today. Enjoy your weekend."

Before Dr. Shehan could even get her last words out, Kimbrel was already packed and standing on her feet. She fastened the buckle on her bag and swung the bag onto her right shoulder. She gave Samyra a glance and said, "Let's go, girl! Time to get out of here!"

Samyra said, "Hold on, girl! Geez! Can I pack my bag?"

Kimbrel giggled. She said, "I can't believe you weren't already packing up when you heard her say, 'I'm dismissing you early.' I started packing right then!"

They both laughed. It really had been a tough week with assignments, projects and labs. Samyra was ready to go, but she wasn't half as ready as Kimbrel obviously was. Once Samyra was packed, they walked out of class and headed downstairs to the parking lot to Samyra's car. It was her week to drive. Kimbrel, Samyra and Jennifer carpooled to and from school each day and the driver rotated every week. This not only helped them save on gas, but it helped each of them save money all around.

Jennifer was already at the car when Kimbrel and Samyra got there. She couldn't believe it took them that long to get to the car after Dr. Shehan's early dismissal.

Jennifer said, "What in the *world* took y'all so long? I was out of there the moment she said *'Enjoy your weekend.'* And I didn't look back!"

Kimbrel laughed and high fived Jennifer. Kimbrel said, " I know that's right! Samyra was the one who was moving like my granny."

Kimbrel and Jennifer laughed with each other.

"I would have been right here with you if it wasn't for her. You know I'm ready to go. I have a fabric shipment waiting on me at the apartment," Kimbrel said with a little dance in her feet.

Samyra said, "You have another shipment? That's the third one this week, isn't it?"

"Yes, yes, yes! It certainly is! I just needed this new fabric so I can finish this outfit I'm working on."

Jennifer chimed in and said, "Girl, you don't get this happy about medical school, but you just keep giving it all your time. Why?"

"You know? I don't even really know," Kimbrel replied. "I really do not know."

It was the first time Kimbrel heard herself say that she didn't know why she was still in medical school. She'd thought it in her mind. She had asked herself a million times, but she was never confronted with the question outside of her own thinking. Saying it out loud did something to her. At that moment, it was like she just couldn't take it anymore. She even whispered it quietly to herself in the back seat while Samyra and Jennifer talked about something else up front. *"Why do I keep going to class and studying and doing all of this stuff when I don't even care?"*

The car pulled up to their apartment complex. They all said a few final words to each other and went their separate ways. Kimbrel walked up to her apartment door and the package she'd been waiting for was there. She picked it up, unlocked her door and stepped into her apartment. Before she could even close the door behind her, the tears were rolling down her face. What had she been doing for the past year and half of her life? She knew she *could* be a doctor, but should she? Why wasn't she as excited as her dad was? Why couldn't she see it his way? Why couldn't she see that brilliant people are supposed to do brilliant things, and why couldn't she be okay with that and just do something brilliant without questioning it? Why would she be so excited about designing and creating clothes when it would probably lead her nowhere? Those were all the questions she fell to her knees and asked God. She couldn't even believe she hadn't asked Him before. Every morning when she would pray and spend time with God in His word, she would tell Him how tired she was and how she wasn't excited anymore, but she would never ask Him if there was something else she should be doing. She never asked Him to show her why she was so tired of medical school. She never asked Him to show her why she was so excited about designing and creating. But she did that day. She had to. It was out in the open, and her heart was breaking over it. She prayed and talked to God. She needed Him to direct her. She needed Him to show her what to do.

"Lord, I don't even know how I ended up here," she started. "I don't know how I loved everything about the medical field one day, but then when I finally get here, I hate it. And I want to be the best that I can be. I want to use the intelligence you gave me so I can be great. I want to use everything you blessed me with to be a blessing to others, but how can I do that in something that just doesn't feel right to me AT ALL? Lord, what do I do from here? I'm so confused, and all I really want is to do what you want me to do. I thought going to medical school was it because my dad said I had to do something where my brains won't go to waste, but Lord, what do you say? Can my brains and my hands be used some other way? If I don't know anything else, Lord, I know medical school is not the way. This can't be what you have for me because what you have for me would be a joy. It wouldn't be a dread. Lord, I'm just asking you to show me. In Jesus' name. Amen."

    Kimbrel stayed there in silence with her tears for about another 10 minutes. Then, she got up from the floor, grabbed the box of fabric that was still next to her, and walked to her sewing room. She dropped the box on the table and then went to the bathroom to take a shower. She just wanted to release all of the different emotions she experienced in the 20 minute span of her getting out of Samyra's car to the time she spent in prayer. The shower helped soothe her; she needed it. After her shower, she went into the sewing room. Now she was *really* about to be at peace. She couldn't wait to see the fabric and hold it in her hands. The outfit she'd started working on 2 weeks prior was finally about to be finished! Kimbrel got everything set up for her to begin working. She opened the playlist on her phone with song after song from her favorite artist, Tye Tribbett, and pressed play. Then she turned the volume up to MAX and worked through the night until it was done.

    It was 11:45 pm when she finished the high-wasted baby doll skirt and a peplum thick-strapped, criss-crossed back tank in different shades of her signature color, pink. She was so proud of it! Finallly, after seeing the outfit in her head for weeks, it was right in front of her. And like she always did, Kimbrel dressed her mannequin with the outfit, took several pictures, created a collage with the pictures and posted the collage on Instagram. After making the official "It's Finished" post, Kimbrel wanted to celebrate the work she did and give herself a little pat on the back, so she went into her kitchen, got a bowl of ice cream and sat on the couch to watch a little TV.

At 1:15 am, Kimbrel heard her phone in the sewing room. She heard the tone that lets her know she has notifications on social media. She didn't hear the tone just once either. She heard it several times. She went to grab it and saw that she had 28 DMs on Instagram. When she opened Instagram to go and read the DMs, she had 135 likes and 82 comments. She couldn't believe it! Kimbrel looked at the time. It was 1:18 am. She looked at the time she posted the picture. 11:52 pm. It hadn't even been 2 hours and the picture had already gotten that much attention. She was freaking out! There were other skirts and tops, dresses and suits and nice pants that she'd spent WAY more time on that didn't get half the likes that that outfit got. Every one of the 28 DMs asked if they could get one just like it. Some asked if they could get it in different sizes and if they could get it in different colors. Kimbrel spent about 20 minutes reading every comment and every DM. She couldn't even respond at that time because she was in shock. She couldn't believe that that many people were interested in the outfit and actually wanted her to make one for them.

She got a few more likes and comments as she was reading everything, but she didn't get anymore DMs. Kimbrel was so excited and so anxiously nervous at the same time, that she didn't think she would be able to sleep. Her body said otherwise, though. It had been a long day and she had worked nonstop on her outfit, so she couldn't keep her eyes opened. She curled up in her bed and was asleep in less than 10 minutes.

In the morning when she woke, her first thought was to pray. She was still excited about the Instagram attention her design had gotten. She thanked God. She told Him, "Lord, I can't believe it! I mean, I was just doing what I love to do and now these people want me to design clothes for them. This is unreal! And I wanna do it, but how can I do that AND do everything medical school requires of me with classes and labs and studying? When will I find the time? Lord, if you make the time in my schedule, I'll do it, and I really wanna do it."

Kimbrel knew she could get it done if she had the time and worked really hard. It didn't take as long to do that outfit as some of her other clothes had, and if she only had 28 to do, she could just make a really tight schedule to get it all in. She asked the Lord again, "Please, Lord, let it fit in my schedule."

She wanted to call Samyra and talk it over with her. She reached for her phone and saw that she had 46 more DMs, for a total of 74! Every one of them was asking to have an outfit just like that one, and it was hard to ignore those requests. She called Samyra and told her everything. They went over every detail, and Samyra was in awe!

Samyra said, "Kim, I think it might be time for you to follow your passion, girl. You were done with medical school pretty much as soon as you got here."

Kimbrel said, "I know. I can't just quit school to sew all these people's clothes. How can I do school AND do this?"

"Well, why can't you just quit school?" Samyra asked in that way that only she could. Every time she used that tone of voice with Kimbrel, it let her know that she meant business.

"Are you serious? Do you really think I would just leave school?" Kimbrel laughed in a high-pitched tone.

"Well, you said yourself that you can't do school and do fashion. How else will you be able to do what you do naturally and what obviously makes you happy if you don't let school go?"

Kimbrel said, "Oh my God, girl! I have never even considered just straight up leaving school."

Samyra said, "Let's look at it this way. We're students. Medical students. We don't make money now because it's impossible for us to have jobs with all the work we do for school. We don't make money until we become doctors. We're living off of our parents and grants and loans. If you start making clothes for people now, you are literally starting your own business and making your own money. If this many people want your clothes now, do you think they're gonna stop wanting them? If they like your work, they will want more of it. And if people are willing to pay, let's run some figures to see how much all of the materials will cost, and how much it will cost to ship the clothes to your customers. With that, we can come up with a price for you to charge."

Kimbrel said, "Yes! Okay. Let's do that! Can you come over now?"

"Give me an hour, girl. I just got up. And didn't you just wake up too? Bye, Kim. Go brush your teeth, nasty!"

Kimbrel laughed and said, "Okay. I'll see you in an hour."

Kimbrel could hardly keep still. She just kept pacing the floor in her living room. To her, when she was creating and designing, it just felt like she was back in her room at her parents' house all those years ago, making clothes for her dolls. She stopped pacing for a minute. She closed her eyes and imagined herself doing one of the many fashion shows she put on for her family in their living room when she was just 10 years old. It didn't feel like work to her. It just felt like she was being Kimbrel. She was just doing what came naturally for her and what excited her and what gave her joy. Now, she had been presented with a way for her to make money while doing it.

Samyra was at Kimbrel's apartment within the hour and they immediately got to work. They started searching out the different fabrics and other materials she would need, and they got prices for everything. They checked to see how much shipping would be by weight first, and then they checked to see how much it would be to different areas of the country and around the world because Kimbrel had gotten two DMs from people in Europe. They even came up with a name for Kimbrel's business: *A Special Design*. They created a business plan that detailed how she could get more people interested in the clothes she makes within the next 3 months, and they projected how much money she would make if that was successful. After all of that, they decided that she would charge $85 for each set. They created a flyer with all of the necessary information and with instructions on how to make orders, and they posted it on Instagram. After only 20 minutes, Kimbrel had 7 orders. And it kept going and going! By the end of the day, she had 80 orders! **(Do the math in the margin of this page.($85 x 80) How much did she make?)** She knew right then that this HAD TO BE God's way of telling her which way to go. It had to be! The joy she felt at that moment, she NEVER felt as a medical student. The fulfillment she got from simply doing what she loved was enough, but to know that it made other people happy *AND* she got paid...THAT was God, and she knew it! Kimbrel didn't hesitate; she made every one of the 80 sets that people ordered from all over the world! And it wasn't easy to do while still in medical school. She had many early mornings and many late nights. She was exhausted most of the time, but she was determined to make the beginning days of her business successful. After she mailed off her last set, she decided, in that very moment, to finish out that year of medical school, but to end it there. She knew she could definitely become a doctor, but she wasn't passionate about being one, and she realized she wasn't passionate about it because she wasn't created for it. Anything she did outside of what she was created to do made her uncomfortable. She was a special design who God created to make special designs for other people. She was created to create. She was created to design. God placed that gift inside of her in her mother's womb. Nobody had to teach her to do it; it came naturally. She could look at a piece of clothing and know exactly how to make it. Color schemes and color patterns just made sense to her. She could talk fashion with the best of them because it was IN her! And because God made her for it, He made a way for her to be prosperous in it. All Kimbrel had to do was be EXACTLY who He created her to be. All she had to do was live out her special design.

A Special Design: Day 1 Study
PURPOSE

Let me tell you something that you might not already know. It's going to blow your mind! Are you ready? Okay. Here goes...

EVERYTHING *that has ever been made has a purpose (reason) for being made.*

Any object, electronic device, and even any store you can think of that we see in our world today was created for a reason. There's *nothing* here that does not have a purpose. **Isn't that amazing?** Let's look at a few examples.

Why do you think God created trees?

_____

_____

Why do you think we have cars in our world?

A Special Design

_____

_____

Why do you think someone created cell phones?

_____

_____

We get so many things from trees! Many of the **foods** we eat come from trees. Trees provide **homes** for birds, mainly, but other creatures form habitation in trees. **Shade** comes from trees and provides cooling for us on hot days. **Furniture, paper, pencils and many other wooded substances** come from trees. And the **oxygen** we need to breathe? Yeah, that's enhanced by trees. See? Trees DEFINITELY have a purpose!

Cars (and other vehicles) provide **transportation**, of course. People walked everywhere before there was any transportation, but thank God someone saw a way for us to get around more quickly! They saw a way for us to save and make the most of time. With the introduction of transportation, people were able to get messages and goods and services more quickly, and now, if we have family members who live far away from us, we can get to them faster. Can you imagine walking from Georgia to Louisiana? That's what I would have to do to see my family. Geesh! Cars DEFINITELY have a purpose!

What *CAN'T* we do with cell phones? They're used for **communication**, allowing us to talk to anyone, anywhere, at any time. And not only can we talk to them, but we can **text, e-mail, and video chat** right from our phones. We're able to stay connected to people. Did you know there was a time when we weren't able to just pick up and call anywhere in the country? There was a time when we had to pay long distance fees to call from state to state. And we couldn't text or write e-mails before cell phones and computers. We hand wrote letters and sent them by postal mail to whoever we wanted to talk to. It took anywhere from 3 days to as long as a week for it to reach the other person. Now it happens in an instant!

And what about that GPS? Thank God for it! I love visiting Atlanta, but I need help getting around. GPS has my back and gets me wherever I need to go. Those cell phones DEFINITELY have purpose!

God himself created the trees. He's the one who gave someone the ability to invent a car, and He gave someone else the ability to create cell phones. All of those things have purpose. And guess what? He created **YOU**, and **YOU** have purpose too!

Read Jeremiah 1:5-8. Sum this passage up in your own words.

_____

_____

A Special Design

_____

_____

Now read Jeremiah 29:11. Sum this scripture up in your own words.

_____

_____

_____

_____

Before you were even born, God set you apart. He knew why He wanted you here and what He wanted you to do before He even created you. I mean, think about it. It makes sense. Henry Seely, the person who invented the iron, knew exactly what he wanted it to do before he created it. He designed the iron in his mind and had all of its details worked out before he created it. The iron was created to solve a problem: remove wrinkles from clothes. Seely saw that problem and created a solution for it. You were created to solve a problem too. Because God already has a plan for you, to give you a future, he knows if you're going to be a doctor and solve health problems. He knows if you're going to be a lawyer and solve legal problems. He knows if you're going to be a cosmetologist and make people more beautiful than they were before they came to you. He knows who you're going to be and what problems He wants you to solve. So guess what He did? He gave you everything you need to be able to do whatever it is He created you for. He equipped you, at birth, for your purpose.

That cell phone was created to do certain things. Cars were created to do certain things. Trees have specific purposes. And YOU... you, my dear, have a specific purpose too.

When God created Kimbrel, He gave her a specific passion and all the skills she would need to work in that passion. What was Kimbrel's passion? What skills did God give her to work in her passion?

_____

_____

_____

_____

_____

I thank God for people like Kimbrel who solve the clothing problems in the world. See, Ms. I. doesn't like to dress up if she doesn't have to. I'm not a tomboy, but I'm not a girly girl either. I like to wear nice clothes, and I DO wear nice clothes, but I don't enjoy shopping for the clothes. If I never had to visit a clothing store again in my life, I'd be just fine. That's where the

A Special Design

Kimbrels of the world come in. They save the day for people like me. When I'm expected to dress up for a particular event, I can see an outfit in my head, and I know how I want to look, but going out to find it is not my idea of fun. I dread it! Kimbrel, who not only designs clothes at a person's request, but sends the clothes directly to the person, is a DREAM for people like me. And again, just like Kimbrel, you were specially created by God with specific gifts and talents that will be a blessing to others. He created you WITH a purpose, FOR a purpose.

Read Psalm 139:13-16. *(One of Ms. I's favorite passages of scripture)*

You are FEARFULLY and WONDERFULLY made, which basically means that you are made exactly the way God intended. He took special care in knitting you together in your mother's womb. And the best part of this passage says that **ALL THE DAYS ORDAINED FOR YOU WERE WRITTEN IN HIS BOOK BEFORE EVEN ONE OF THEM CAME TO BE!** That just makes me happy! I get excited when I read that and when I'm reminded that the Lord had a plan for me **BEFORE** He even created me. And because He knows what He wants me to do, He carefully equipped me with the personality, the skills, and the ability to do everything He created me to do. My personality is just right for what I was created to do. My natural skills are just right for what I was created to do. Even my quirks are just right for what I was created to do. And the same is true for you. You are just right for everything that God created you to do!

Read Ephesians 2:10. What does this verse say about you?

Stories THAT TEACH Girls

_____

_____

Think about an architect, a carpenter, and a builder. When they design and create things, they usually have a signature style that lets people know it's their work. They don't have to sign their name to it. They don't have to post a picture of themselves next to their work. They don't have to stand by and tell people that they created whatever it is they created. Their style is so uniquely theirs that people just know whenever something is created by them. Food is the same way. *(I would know. I LOVE to eat! Ha!)* Both *Popeye's* and *Church's* are known for their fried chicken, but their chicken doesn't taste the same. Most anyone who's ever had chicken from both places could do a blind taste test and easily tell which chicken was *Popeye's* and which chicken was *Church's*. Each restaurant has a unique recipe. Each architect, each carpenter, and each builder has a unique "recipe" too. Their workmanship, or their creative style is unique. And guess what God is saying to you? "You, _____ **(write your first name)**, *are MY workmanship! You were created in MY image with supernatural skills, talents, and abilities that I wanted specifically for you. No one had to teach you to do what you do because I gave it to you, and no one can take it away from you. And like Ephesians 2:10 says, I prepared work, in advance, for you to do. When people see you doing that work, they'll know you're MY workmanship. You carry my signature design. You are my specially made recipe to solve a specific problem in the earth."*

A Special Design

Read Matthew 10:30. Write it below.

_____

_____

If you ever wonder... If you ever forget... If you ever doubt that God created you on purpose for a purpose, remind yourself of what Matthew 10:30 says. It says that the very hairs on your head are numbered. Now, let me break that down for you. Because God created you, He can look at your head and say, *"She has 33, 987 hairs on her head,"* but He could also lift one string of hair and say, *"That's number 889."* Woo! That's powerful! That's how intimately He knows you. He knows EVERYTHING about you because He was intentional in creating you just the way He wanted you.

There's something for you to do that will help people and make their lives easier. Who knows? You may be the doctor who delivers my child one day. You may be the lawyer or the accountant on the Praise Movement School of Dance staff that handles all of our legal and business affairs as we travel the country and teach girls. Just know that **your purpose is <u>already</u> in you!**

Did you know before today that you were created ON PURPOSE, FOR A PURPOSE?

YES   NO

If you answered YES, how did you know? Did you learn anything new about YOU today?

_____

_____

_____

_____

If you answered NO, explain what you learned about YOU today.

_____

_____

_____

_____

A Special Design: Day 2 Study
MINISTRY, PART 1

Years ago, I prayed and asked the Lord to give me a simple definition of the word *ministry*. I knew what it was, but I wanted to explain it to my young dancers in a way that they could understand. Year after year, girls would come to Praise Movement Summer Dance Camp and not know what ministry was, so before we could tell them to minister as they danced, we had to first teach them what that meant. Most of them believed that ministry could only be done at church, and some believed that only pastors could do ministry. I HAD TO clear that up! There was no way I was going to let them leave believing any of those things.

In my quiet time one day, the Lord gave me a definition. He said ministry is **using our gifts, talents, and abilities to tell someone else about Jesus**—His death on a cross, His burial, and His resurrection for US so that we can have eternal life with God. We use our gifts talents and abilities to tell others that Jesus is the way, the truth, and the life, and that no one goes to the Father except through Him. (John 14:6)

Highlight (or underline) the definition of ministry.

I was so excited because I knew the girls would understand it. They did, and every year, they do. I also teach them that the best way to do ministry is to do it inside of the purpose for which they were created.

Let me explain.

Stories THAT TEACH Girls

I'm a schoolteacher. Without a doubt, God purposed for me, in my mother's womb, to be a teacher, and I ALWAYS knew I'd be a teacher. My favorite pastime as a child was playing school. *(No one can tell this story like my mom!)*

Sure, I went outside to play sometimes, but I would much rather be in my bedroom, teaching my dolls and imaginary students what I had learned from my teachers in school. And teaching them, although they couldn't hear a word I said, came naturally; I just knew what to do. I LOVED (and still love) school SO much that I played school just about every day. Year after year, without my even knowing so, I was learning from my teachers how to teach my future students. I had great teachers whose skills, love and compassion I later emulated *(Thanks, Mrs. Winkler and Mr. Riley)*, and I had bad teachers whose practices and show-up-to-get-my-paycheck attitudes I vowed to never adopt as my own. Both the good and bad teachers sharpened my natural ability and caused me to grow. When I later joined different clubs and organizations inside and outside of school, it was natural for me to take on leadership roles because that meant I had to show people the ropes. I had to instruct and guide them. If I knew how to do ANYTHING, I could teach anyone else how to do it, and I loved it! My teaching skills were sharpened through those experiences, and with every experience, I became a better teacher.

Then, I went to college to "learn how" to be a teacher because I needed to have the professional credentials to be able to teach in a school. I breezed through classes! Every class was only teaching me how to be the me that I already was. Nothing was difficult. Nothing was hard to understand. Nothing challenged me beyond what I could handle. The teacher was already in me! I was born to teach! By the time I stepped foot into my first classroom as a young adult, I was ready!

So since ministry is using my **gifts, talents** and **abilities** to tell someone else about Jesus, what do you think I should be using? YES! I should be teaching! Teaching **IS** my natural gift, the one (of many) God gave me when He created me. Teaching is what I should be using to tell others about Jesus, or to do ministry. If I'm using my gifts to do ministry, I am fulfilling my **purpose (the reason God created me).**

I am being exactly who God created me to be, and I'm doing exactly what He created me to do.

Think about what you do well. Think about how you're naturally gifted. *(Most people have multiple natural gifts.)* **Remember that you were created for a purpose, so God intentionally gave you certain gifts because there are specific things He wants you to do. List every gift of yours that you can think of. You will use this list later this week, so be sure to list them all!**

_____

_____

_____

_____

Stories THAT TEACH Girls

Had you even heard the word *ministry* before today?

YES   NO

If YES, did today's lesson help you better understand what you already know about the word *ministry*? Explain your understanding of the word *ministry*.

_____

_____

_____

If NO, explain what you understand about the word *ministry* after today's lesson.

_____

_____

_____

A Special Design: Day 3 Study
MINISTRY, PART 2

We learned a lot on Day 1 and Day 2. We know we were created ON purpose FOR a purpose. We know our gifts, and we know what ministry is. We know we should be using our gifts for ministry. Now we need to know WHY we're even doing ministry in the first place. **Why is ministry so important? Why should I even be concerned with telling others about Jesus?** Good questions! I'm glad you asked. ☺

A wise man once told me that the last words someone says are the words they want you to remember most. And it's true. It happens in public speaking, and it happens in writing. It even happens on phone calls when you know you have to hang up. You may say something like, *"And pleeease don't forget to bring the stuff I left at your house to school tomorrow! Pleeease!"* Those last words are the most important to you. Sure, you said things earlier up in the conversation that you want your listener to remember, but you felt the need to say those last words one more time because it's the last thing they'll hear, and it matters more than everything else you said. In the following passage of scripture, Jesus gives His disciples some final words before He ascends into heaven to sit at the right hand of God. These words, since He said them last, must be a pretty big deal.

And Jesus came and spoke to them saying, "All authority has been given Me in heaven and on earth. Go therefore and **<u>make disciples</u>** *of all the nations, baptizing them in the name of the Father and of the Son and of the Holy Spirit,* **<u>teaching them to observe all things that I have commanded you</u>**, *and lo, I am with you always , even to the end of* *the age. Amen."* - ***Matthew 28:18-20 KJV (underlining and bold added for emphasis)***

He left them with a very important assignment. After everything He said to them in the conversation, He made SURE to say those words last. It's what mattered the most. He commissioned (commanded) them to make *disciples*—believers, followers, students (of Jesus)—in all the world, just as He had made them. He told them to teach the new disciples everything He'd taught them and to be encouraged by knowing He'd be with them in their hearts. In this passage, Jesus is speaking directly to His disciples, but this passage, and every other passage like it, is just as much for today's disciples (Christians) as it was for the disciples of that time. Christians are to go into all the earth and make more disciples. THAT'S IT! The disciples back then are the reason why we have disciples (Christians) now. Our job is to make sure there are disciples after us. We are to teach others everything Jesus taught. And here's the good part...

GOD GAVE ALL OF US DIFFERENT GIFTS AND TALENTS TO GET IT DONE!

You get to be EXACTLY who you are and use the gifts He gave you to make disciples! Isn't that great? That's an EASY mission: **Just be YOU and use your gifts to tell others about Jesus! Use your gifts to make disciples.**

We all have our individual purposes where we use our gifts and talents, but ***our purpose as Christians*** is to use those gifts and talents to lead others to relationship with Jesus and make disciples. That's ***ministry***. And Jesus' last, most important words to us were to remind us to do that. This is what we're on this earth to do. We are to make disciples so we can all one day live in heaven with our God. Whatever gifts and talents you've been given, you should be using them for ministry.

Read 1 Peter 4:10-11. Write verse 10 below.

_____

_____

All God ever wants is for you to be the you He created you to be, and use the gifts He gave you FOR OTHERS. When you do that, 1 Peter 4:10 says that God will be praised. When we do something well, it "speaks" to others and causes them to pay attention. When Kimbrel used her natural gift to create and design, people took notice. When I teach my students in school, people sometimes wonder how I get them to understand such difficult concepts and how I get them to do as well as they do. When I teach dance, the same thing happens. It amazes people that I can get a group of dancers to learn so quickly and present so well to an audience or a congregation. When someone plays sports well, the world takes notice. When someone sings well, the world takes notice. When *you* do what God gifted *you* to do, it will cause people to pay attention, and when they do, it points glory to the God who gave you the gift. When you're being you and you're good at being you, others are attracted to the God in you. That gives Him glory and opens the door for you to tell them about Him.

Stories THAT TEACH Girls

Now, let's recap. Answer the following in your own words.

1. God had a reason for creating you, so that means you have a

   _____.

2. What is ministry?

   _____

   _____

   _____

3. Why should you do ministry?

   _____

   _____

   _____

4. What is a disciple?

   _____

5. Why is it important for you to make disciples?

   _____

   _____

   _____

6. What do you believe God is saying to your heart right now about your gifts and ministry? Write it below.

   _____

   _____

   _____

   _____

Stories THAT TEACH *Girls*

A Special Design: Day 4
PROVERBS STUDY

Read Proverbs 22:29 NIV and Proverbs 18:16 KJV. Summarize them below.

_____

_____

_____

_____

_____

    The book of wisdom says that when you're skilled in your work, you will serve before kings. In other words, when you're good at what you do, it will take you to the top and MAKE ROOM FOR YOU in "major" places with "major" people. When you work in your gifting, it will open doors for you. There are many who have already experienced this by simply doing what they were created to do. Let's take *American Idol*, *The Voice*, and *Sunday Best* for example, where regular, everyday people like you and me go and audition to showcase their singing ability. Because they're so good at what they do, they're chosen as finalists to appear on these shows, and just like that, they are seen by millions of people, week in and week out. Some of them, by the end of the competition, get record deals even if they don't win the competition! That's all because the excellence of their natural ability was showcased before the world, and when excellence is showcased on a large scale like that, it's hard to ignore! Because they're so good, they are taken to the top, just like Proverbs 22:29 says they would be. They get to serve (use their gifts) before kings (on a large platform that reaches more people).

And being seen worldwide is not the only way God can open doors and make room for you. What if you are a superior math student, and every day at school you're simply being you, cranking out A's on every assignment.

Your teacher sees your love and enthusiasm for math, but she also sees others in your class who aren't confident in their ability to do math. Your teacher believes those students would benefit from one of their peers working with them on a one-on-one basis, so she decides to make you a peer tutor. You LOVE the idea, and you take it on with much excitement. You do so well at tutoring your peers that you are asked to be a peer tutor in your math class the following school year. That school year, word about you gets around to all of the math teachers, so one day you're called into the office where your math teacher, two other math teachers in the school and your principal are seated at a round table awaiting your arrival. They explain that your outstanding achievement in math and your ability to instruct and guide other students helped bring the school's math scores up dramatically. Since you were working one on one with so many students, and in small groups with others, it gave teachers the ability to work more closely with other students. They express their appreciation for your willingness to serve your fellow students and thank you over and over again. Your principal then asks if you'd be willing to offer your time as Lead Tutor of the peer tutoring program the school plans to implement the following school year. You would not only be responsible for tutoring students, but you would be responsible for scheduling tutoring sessions and assigning other tutors to students who need help. You would earn well beyond the number of hours you'd need for the community service graduation requirement, and if you maintained the A average you maintained in all of your math classes throughout high school so far, you'd be exempt from all exams. Of course, you accept!

Without complaints, you diligently use your natural gift to serve others for three years at your school while maintaining A's in all of your classes, so at graduation you're offered a full scholarship to the college you've always known you wanted to attend. And if having your college education totally funded wasn't enough, your principal announces to everyone at the graduation that you have an on-campus job already waiting for you that will pay $500 a week. *(That's more money than a first-year college student could even dream of! Trust me!)* He goes on to explain that you will continue to serve as a tutor because you love it so much, but you will also serve as Director of Math Tutoring for a team of 10 tutors.

You see, the math teacher you had your 10th grade year who made you a peer tutor would be leaving your high school to take a job as head of the math department at the college you plan to attend. She knew how things were set up at the college. She knew that there would be a tutoring department of some kind. She knew the department would need tutors, and she knew they'd offer scholarships to anyone who could serve in a director position. What she didn't know was that she would not only oversee the 26 math teachers in the department, but she would also be responsible for the 3 math labs on campus that offer tutoring. That meant she had to hire the directors for the 3 math labs. As soon as she knew she had the job, months before your high school graduation, she started looking to hire 3 directors. She wanted people who would work as unto the Lord and not man. She wanted people who genuinely enjoyed teaching others and seeing them get better. She wanted people who knew how to lovingly manage others. She wanted people who would love doing their job. There was no doubt in her mind that you would be one of them.

She never told you she was watching you with the intention of hiring you as a director because she didn't want you to work just because there would be a reward at the end. She was already behind the scenes working everything out for you so you could just show up and do what you love. And that's exactly what you did! You showed up on your new college campus as the Director of Math Tutoring, and every day, you do what you are naturally gifted to do. You get to do what you love.

And this is the way God is with us. When we are simply doing what He's gifted (told) us to do, He is behind the scenes finding or creating platforms for our gifts to be used on a greater level. And it's never really about us. It's always so more people can be blessed by what we have, and ultimately so they can know Jesus and develop a relationship with Him.

As a final reminder, write Proverbs 22:29 and Proverbs 18:16 below.

_____

_____

Stories That Teach Girls

A SPECIAL DESIGN

A Special Design: Day 5
CHALLENGE/ACTIVITY

Have you ever taken the time to *really* look at "who" you are and what you can do? Sure, you made a list of your natural gifts a few days ago, but let's really look at that list. Today, you're going to dig deeper into your natural gifts, talents, and abilities.

Complete the chart. Try your best to discuss *3* of your gifts/talents/skills.

Refer to the following pages for examples...

Gift/Talent/Skill	On a scale of 1-5, how much do you enjoy using this gift/talent/skill? (1=little excitement; 5=much excitement)	What have others said about you when they see you using this gift/talent/skill?	How can you use this gift/talent/skill to help others and/or tell them about Jesus?

Stories THAT TEACH Girls

Gift/Talent/Skill	On a scale of 1-5, how much do you enjoy using this gift/talent/skill? *(1=little excitement; 5=much excitement)*	What have others said about you when they see you using this gift/talent/skill?	How can you use this gift/talent/skill to help others and/or tell them about Jesus?
Ms. I's Example Dance & Choreography	5	My family always told me I danced well. My dance teachers always promoted me to captain because of my skill. Every time I performed, even strangers would tell my family how good I was. I would choreograph too, and the teams I danced with thought my choreography was good.	I can create dances to music that uplifts the name of Jesus and teach it to girls. I can teach them that they're dancing to "speak" the word of God to others. I can teach them that their movements ARE their words and that they do ministry (or not) every time they dance.

A Special Design

Gift/Talent/Skill	On a scale of 1-5, how much do you enjoy using this gift/talent/skill? *(1=little excitement; 5=much excitement)*	What have others said about you when they see you using this gift/talent/skill?	How can you use this gift/talent/skill to help others and/or tell them about Jesus?
Kimbrel's Example Fashion Designing	5	My friends have encouraged me from DAY 1 to design rather than go to school to be a doctor. They LOVE my clothes and social media does too! Strangers compliment me often and ask where my clothes come from.	Since my clothes are always classy, I can encourage women to dress respectably and to respect the body that God gave them. I can remind them that they are His workmanship and that they should always dress the part. I can remind them that they are a reflection of He who made them.

Stories THAT TEACH Girls

Gift/Talent/Skill	On a scale of 1-5, how much do you enjoy using this gift/talent/skill? *(1=little excitement; 5=much excitement)*	What have others said about you when they see you using this gift/talent/skill?	How can you use this gift/talent/skill to help others and/or tell them about Jesus?
Your Example #1			

A Special Design

Gift/Talent/Skill	On a scale of 1-5, how much do you enjoy using this gift/talent/skill? *(1=little excitement; 5=much excitement)*	What have others said about you when they see you using this gift/talent/skill?	How can you use this gift/talent/skill to help others and/or tell them about Jesus?
Your Example #2			

Stories THAT TEACH Girls

Gift/Talent/Skill	On a scale of 1-5, how much do you enjoy using this gift/talent/skill? *(1=little excitement; 5=much excitement)*	What have others said about you when they see you using this gift/talent/skill?	How can you use this gift/talent/skill to help others and/or tell them about Jesus?
Your Example #3			

A Special Design

*Maybe those boxes were too small. Maybe you want to dig deeper into all of your gifts. Here's an extra sheet of paper for you to do that. Break down your gifts as much as you need to, however you need to.

Stories THAT TEACH _girls_

A Special Design: Day 6
GODLY REWARDS

Think back to the Proverbs Study. Proverbs 22:29 reminds us that those who are skilled in their work will serve before kings (go to the top). That is one of God's rewards for simply doing what He tells us to do, being who He created us to be, and using the gifts that He gave us to use. And He not only rewards us by allowing us to rise to the top, but He rewards us by taking care of the things that concern us. He makes sure we have EVERYTHING we need to continue doing what He created us to do.

All Kimbrel did was finally "answer the call" in her heart to do what she was naturally gifted to do. God created her to design and make clothing. She wasn't doing that with her whole heart at first because she thought she should be a doctor. She was miserable in medical school. Going to class and studying for tests wasn't fun. It felt like extra work to her. But when she was designing and making clothes, she was different. That's when she felt alive. She could spend hours and hours designing and creating and never get tired. The joy she experienced when she was doing what God created her to do was unmatched by anything else. When she finally gave up on everything else to just do what she naturally excelled at, God opened up a door for her to not only do what she loves FULL TIME, but He caused her to make money too! She was able to buy more equipment and more material to make more clothes. She had everything she needed to continue doing what the Lord created her to do. She could have made a lot of money as a doctor, but she wouldn't have peace. She would be miserable. She would make just as much money doing what she loved AND, on top of the money, she would have joy and peace. God rewarded her with her own business and she wasn't even trying to have one. She was just being who she was created to be.

Have you ever heard of *Pinky Promise* and/or its founder, Heather Lindsey? If you haven't, look Heather and *Pinky Promise* up on social media. She has a unique story. She wanted to encourage women to honor God with their bodies and with their lives, so she started making and selling bracelets with encouraging messages on them. She wanted women to see the messages on their wrists and remember that they belonged to the Lord. From the bracelets came a movement. Heather knew that the bracelets weren't enough to make women honor the Lord with their bodies and their lives. They needed God's word in their hearts for that. She began a network of small groups so she could encourage women with the word of God, and today there are hundreds of groups all over the United States and in other countries. She hosts an annual *Pinky Promise* conference for thousands of women, and she's written several books to encourage women to continue to live lives that please the Lord. Heather will be the first to tell you, as she's said on many occasions, that she wasn't looking to start a business. She was simply doing what she believed the Lord was telling her to do. She was just being who He created her to be and encouraging women like He told her to, and BAM! It grew, and He took her to the top. People all over the world are encouraged by her because she simply does what He says do. He rewarded her with her businesses that help take care of her family, but more importantly, He allows her to make money through those businesses so she can have everything she needs to continue in MINISTRY. He takes care of her, so she can take care of His people. This is how God rewards.

Stories THAT TEACH Girls

In August 2004, the Lord gave me the plan for Praise Movement Summer Dance Camp because He knew dance was what He gifted me to do. I was excited about the plan because I wanted the opportunity to teach girls the word of God, and' I wanted to teach it through dance. I was getting the opportunity to be who He created me to be, and to use the gifts He gave me. The first camp was held in July 2005. I wasn't even planning a camp in 2006 because I thought my work was done; I had done what the Lord told me to do, but the families of the girls who participated in 2005 were looking forward to the following year. Pretty much everyone was talking about who they were planning to bring the next summer and how they couldn't wait until the next summer. I couldn't believe it! I knew then that it had to go forth because God wanted to continue the work. In 2006, more girls came. In 2007, even more girls came. Before I knew it, there were girls from all over the city of Augusta learning the word of God through dance, and they were excited about teaching others. Without me even trying, Praise Movement became a business. It had to! I was managing so many different components of the dance camp ministry that we needed more hands and more resources. Soon, Praise Movement was being asked to minister in different places throughout the year, and the dance camp grew like crazy and got bigger and bigger every summer! In 2014, the Lord gave me the plan for a dance tour, where the Praise Movement dancers and I would go into different cities and teach God's word with dance. We've been on 3 fall tours and next year, we plan to add a spring tour. It has been amazing to watch God provide money and resources for dance camp every summer and for every dance tour. We always have EVERYTHING we need for EVERYTHING He tells us to do. This is how God rewards.

Because of Praise Movement's growth, I'm asked on a regular basis to either help start, or help develop dance ministries at different churches. I'm often asked to teach the girls the importance of honoring God with their bodies and to instruct them on how to dance unto the Lord. I facilitate workshops all over the city of Augusta and in surrounding areas, and all I'm doing is being me. As a result, so many girls know who Jesus is and have given their hearts to Him. God has rewarded me and keeps rewarding me because I do what He tells me to do. He gave me the gifts of dance and teaching so I can make disciples, and as long as I'm doing that, He will make sure I have what I need to do it.

There are SO MANY other examples out there of people who are simply doing what the Lord tells them to do and who are being who He created them to be. They are being rewarded too.

Let's look at someone from God's word, Joseph, who used his natural gift to help someone else. Because of it, he served before a king and was rewarded by God. Joseph, at the time of this story, was imprisoned, and had been for quite some time. During his imprisonment, two men who were in the same prison had dreams that they couldn't understand. God gave Joseph the natural ability to interpret dreams, so he was able to tell the men what their dreams meant. The two men were eventually released from the prison, and Joseph asked one of the men to remember what he'd done for him. Joseph wanted the man to speak to Pharoah (the king) for him so he, too, could be released from the prison, but the man forgot about Joseph. It wasn't until 2 years later when the king had 2 dreams that he didn't understand that Joseph would be released.

Read Genesis 41:1-45 to see what happened next.

No one in the kingdom could interpret the king's dreams, so the king had his officials to search for someone who could. It was at that moment that the man from the prison remembered Joseph. He told the king that Joseph could interpret his dreams. The king sent for Joseph, and Joseph heard the king's dreams. When Joseph was asked to interpret the dreams, Joseph said, *"I cannot do it, but God will give Pharaoh the answer he desires." (verse 16)*

Joseph was sure to let the king know that it wasn't in his ability or in his own strength that he was able to interpret the dreams. It was a gift that God gave him, and he wouldn't be able to tell him anything apart from his relationship with, and connection to God. Joseph would tell Pharoah what the dreams meant, but it would be God's interpretation.

After explaining the dreams, Joseph even told the king what he should do to prepare for what the dreams had shown him. The king was so pleased with what Joseph had done for him! He said, *"Can we find anyone like this man, one in whom is the spirit of God?"(verse 38)* The king knew that the Lord had given Joseph the ability to interpret the dreams and the wisdom to know what to do about the dreams. The king could see God's gifting working in Joseph. The king said, *"Since God has made all this known to you, there is no one so discerning and wise as you." (verse 39)* And just like that, Joseph was placed in a position of power over EVERYONE...even the officials and other servants that had spent years with the king had to answer to Joseph! He was...

1. put in charge of the king's palace. The WHOLE palace! *(Imagine an apartment complex to envision the size of a palace.) (verse 40)*

2. made the overseer of all of the kings subjects (every helper and servant throughout the palace). (verse 40)

3. put in charge of the whole land of Egypt! (verse 41)

Pharoah took his official kingly ring and placed it on Joesph's finger *(This was a BIG DEAL back then)*. He dressed him in fine clothing and put a gold chain on his neck. The king then paraded Joseph around in his chariot as his second-in-command and gave him a wife, which was considered a man's highest favor. (verses 41-45) If he was given a wife, he was blessed. God rewarded Joseph GREATLY for being who He created Him to be, and using the gifts that He gave him to use.

You, my dear, don't have time to waste with being someone God didn't create you to be. Your wealth, your favor, your blessings...EVERYTHING you need is in the YOU that God created. When you're trying to be someone else, you're missing what God has for YOU. The Lord has promised in His word that you will serve (use your gifts) before kings (on a large platform) if you are skilled at your work, and when He gave you your gifts, you were automatically skilled. We have a responsibility to sharpen our skills to be good at what we do, but we already have all we need. You're not designed to serve before obscure (unnoticeable, unimportant) men, like the verse says. You were made to serve at the top so others can know who your God is and honor Him!

Revisit this study and your chart from yesterday when it's time for you to choose a major in college or a job. Revisit this when you're looking to see what it is you want to do with the rest of your life. When you're looking for a career, see where you can use who you naturally are, if the Lord doesn't completely create something just for you before then!

A Special Design: Day 7

JOURNAL

Remember that God wants you to be who HE made you and to use what HE gave you for ministry (to make disciples). When others see you being great, it brings glory to Him because you're HIS workmanship. Sometimes, when we're not even trying, we speak about the God who created us, but He DOES want us to be intentional about using "who" we are to show others who He is.

Can you think of someone who uses their gifts, talents and abilities to tell others about Jesus? Do you know anyone (or know of anyone) who is making disciples simply by being who God created them to be? Write about that person (those people). What do they do? How are they using their gifts?

_____

_____

_____

_____

_____

The White Scarf

by Iantha Ussin (Ms. I.)

Stories That Teach Girls

Alahna is 15 and at the end of her sophomore year in high school. She is her parents' only daughter. Her parents thought they would NEVER have a daughter after having four boys, so when Alahna finally came along, she immediately became the center of attention, especially for her mother who always, always, always wanted a daughter. From birth, Alahna was the apple of her mother's eye. She wanted to give Alahna everything that she never had, and she wanted to teach her things early in life—those things that took her until her old age to learn. She felt Alahna deserved her very best.

Now, Alahna's mother was a famous seamstress and personal fashion stylist for music artists, actors, and actresses that we all know and love. Her clients loved her and were faithful to her because not only was she really good at what she did, but she used fabrics and garments from exotic countries—the best of everything, right down to buttons and zippers—to make her clothes.

Alahna, of course, had been having clothes made for her from birth. Her christening gown was laced in authentic white pearls from Japan. Every year for her birthday, she had a dress specially made according to the theme of her birthday party. One year, the year she turned 10, she had an Aladdin theme, so of course, she was dressed as Princess Jasmine, and her fabric and jewelry was hand-picked and imported from Arabia. Her mother always knew, though, that she would do something special for her 13th birthday—something that went beyond the party and the clothes. She wanted something to commemorate her daughter stepping into her teenage years that she would remember and could keep for years to come, because this was the tradition in their family. Alahna's great-grandmother, Leola, gave her grandmother, Sadie, her wedding band to wear on her ring finger until she got married. After Sadie got married, she could either wear it on her right hand or give it to *her* daughter. Sadie decided to keep it and give Alahna's mother, Gwendolyn, the pin that she used to close up the front of her blouse when she and Alahna's grandfather went on their first date. Alahna's mother designed her own wedding dress, of course, so she made that pin a part of the design of the dress, right at the center of her chest, just like her mom had worn it. So passing the pin down to Alahna was out of the question.

Alahna's mother, Gwen is what everyone called her, decided to make Alahna a scarf that she would use to wipe away her tears of joy on her wedding day. Gwen researched some Parisian fabrics and cloth that she had never used before because for this, she wouldn't dare use anything that she had used for someone else, and she would never use it again for anyone. This was especially for her Alahna. The pure white cloth was imported from Paris. She lined it with a fine silver threading that she had gotten on a trip to the Virgin Islands, but never saw fit to use for any of her clients. She lined the scarf from corner to corner with petite pearls from the coasts of Africa, and she finished it, as she did all of her creations by etching her initials in one of the corners—G.O.D.—Gwendolyn Olivia Davenport.

She designed a plastic case, initials and all, for Alahna to keep the cloth in. When Alahna was presented with her gift on her 13th birthday, she knew it was precious and sacred not only because of the fine materials her mother used to make it just for her, but because her mother shared with her, once again, the significance of the tradition that the women in the family had kept for several generations. Alahna kept her scarf in her top drawer and looked forward to wiping her tears of joy on her wedding day.

Now, as Alahna got older, she was just as much into fashion as her mother. She especially loved accessorizing her outfits, and she did it well. She even helped her friends with their wardrobes. She always knew what hat would go well with an outfit, and what shoes matched what jewelry. And there had been several times in her fashion sessions when she would be putting an outfit together, and she would look in her drawers for scarves or undershirts or whatever and would see her wedding day scarf. A few times, she thought that it would go PERFECTLY with something she was wearing, especially with the silver lining that would be JUST RIGHT with her silver jewelry, but she treasured her scarf too much to use if for anything other than what her mother, the one who made it, said it should be used for.

Alahna's style of dress got her much attention! And as an up and coming junior, she had to make sure her look was always top notch. One guy in particular, Sa'Tahn, noticed her like no one else had. He had been watching her all school year. He liked how she always had the shoes and jewelry to match, and he always told his boys, *"That's just attractive to me. I like how Alahna be rockin' it."*

Alahna got accustomed to Sa'Tahn watching her EVERY TIME she passed him in the hall, and she began to look for the smiles and head nods he directed toward her. When she knew she'd get that attention from him, it made her work a little bit longer and a little bit harder on making that outfit just right. She wondered, though, if he was ever going to try and talk to her. She DEFINITELY wasn't going to say anything to him. Her daddy would tell her over and over again, *"Lahna, baby, you don't ever chase or throw yourself at a brotha cuz that's the one girl he don't want. To him, that girl is too easy. A man likes a challenge. The more he has to work for you and the more he has to wait for you, the more he will want to be with you. Be mysterious, baby. Make him wonder about you. Don't show him everything you have the moment you meet him."*

The end-of-the-year school dance was swiftly approaching, and like always, Alahna and her girl, Talia, were going. Alahna had been working on her outfit for months, and she was ready, but there was just something missing—the UMPH that she was accustomed to having. The day of the dance, for the fiftieth time, she went through all of her threads and rags and scarves, for she had VERY many, but she couldn't find anything. She went into her jewelry box to pick out the silver jewelry she needed to match the stones in the shirt that her mom designed for her. She kept thinking in her head, *"This outfit just ain't giving me what I need. If I just had something silver to go around my waist..."* And BAM! The moment she thought silver, the silver lining in her wedding day scarf started flashing in her mind.

Every day going in and out of her top drawer, she never even noticed the scarf. It was just simply out of the question. She wouldn't be seeing that scarf go to use until she was married 10 or so years down the road, but for the first time, it had some real appeal. All she could think about was the compliments she would get, and especially the ones she might get from Sa'Tahn. She could see the complete outfit in her mind, and she KNEW if she wore that scarf and made it look like a belt, it was on!

Alahna felt nervous about even taking the scarf out of its plastic case. It was so clean, so perfect, so pure; it had literally never been touched. She looked at it for a while and thought that even though it was made for one purpose, it wouldn't hurt to just wear it and put it back after this one outfit. She wasn't accustomed to wearing things twice anyway. She started thinking. "Well, I don't dance at dances so I don't have to worry about sweating, and I plan to eat and drink at home before I go, so that takes care of me spilling anything on it."

And just like that, her decision was made. She was definitely wearing the scarf.

Alahna walked a few houses down to Talia's house with the plastic case in her purse. For all social events, Talia's parents dropped the girls off, and Alahna's parents picked them up. She waited until she got to Talia's house to put on her finishing touch, and it worked beautifully!

When they got to the dance, Alahna's outfit was, of course, as usual, the center of attention. Sa'Tahn watched her all night, but he waited until the end of the dance to walk over to Alahna and tell her how good she looked. And he *finally* asked her for her number. They walked outside together to wait on their parents to pick them up.

They talked about some different things for a little bit and Sa'Tahn said, "I need something to remember you by from tonight."

He unhooked his cross necklace and pulled it from around his neck. He said, "You can hold this til' tomorrow so you can remember me."

Alahna said, "I don't have nothin' for you."

Sa'Tahn said, "You ain't gon' let me hold *nothin*'? I'm just sayin'. I can't put yo ring on my pinky?" He pointed to Alahna's platinum band, the one her grandmother gave her at her Coming of Age Ceremony that their church has for boys and girls when they turn 13.

Sa'Tahn continued, "You got this fly belt on too. I need to be sleepin' with that under my pillow."

"Boy, you play too much!" Alahna giggled and gave Sa'Tahn a shy side eye. "You ain't gettin' my stuff. And it's a scarf anyway. It's not a belt."

"See, that's why I like you. You be makin' scarves look like belts and stuff. That's what I'm talkin' bout!"

Sa'Tahn moved from standing beside Alahna so he could stand face to face with her and said, "What you gon' do? You know I'ma be at the park tomorrow, so you can just bring my chain and I'll bring yo belt."

"What time you gon' be at the park?" Alahna asked with an unsure smile.

Sa'Tahn smacked his teeth, stepped back with one foot, and cocked his head up to the right so he could look at Alahna out of the side of his eye. He said, "You know what time I'm out there every Saturday. Don't even front like that. You and ya girls be out there."

She was thinking about it. She saw that her scarf had been in PERFECT condition all night. She knew it would be back in the plastic case just like new if she just put it back right then. Everybody was pretty much gone, and they had already seen her outfit, so she wanted to just put it back in her purse. But Sa'Tahn walked around her, hugged her from behind, and whispered in her ear, "So what you gon' do boo? Don't make me go home without nothin'? I'ma have it at the park, and when I call you tonight, I'ma let you know it's alright. I'ma take good care of it. And you betta take good care of my chain too, girl."

He was holding on to the scarf around her waist. She was SO gone with him hugging her and whispering in her ear that she didn't even notice he was grabbing onto her scarf. All she knew was she was finally getting the attention from Sa'Tahn that she always wanted.

She said, "Alright, 'Tahn. I'm not playin'. My scarf betta come back to me just like I give it to you."

She reached into her purse and pulled out the plastic case with her mother's initials on it and said, "And, here. Put it in here to keep it clean."

"Uh oh!" Sa'Tahn said with a sly chuckle. He was impressed. "You got cases for your belts? Girl, you gon' be takin' care of me like that when we get married, huh?"

Alahna heard the word married and her heart skipped a beat. She had been in another world, but hearing that word brought her back to reality. That *WAS* what her mom had made the scarf for, wasn't it? She grabbed the case from Sa'Tahn, took the scarf from around her waist, and put it in the case herself. She looked at him, and marriage kept ringing in her head. Her mom said it was for her to wipe her tears of joy on her wedding day, and here she was in front of her school, wiping the scarf between his and her sweaty hands. Sa'Tahn reached out his hand, but Alahna held on.

Sa'Tahn said, "What's up with my belt, boo?"

Alahna paused for a moment. She looked at Sa'Tahn, then she looked at her feet. She looked back up at Sa'Tahn, and he gave her that grin that he always gave her when he would see her in the halls at school. She looked back at her feet. Then she stepped back to create a space between them and said, "You know what? Let me give you your chain back."

She put the case with her scarf in it back in her purse so she could free up both of her hands. She grabbed the hook on the chain at the back of her neck and unfastened it. As she took it from around her neck, she looked at Sa'Tahn. His eyes were wide open just staring at her as she took it off.

Sa'Tahn said, "Hold uuuuuuup! Hold up, boo!"

He put his hands on her hands and tried to take the chain and put it back around her neck. He said, "Why you took it off?"

With tears forming in her eyes, Alahna said, "I can't give you my scarf, boy. You don't even know how messed up I would be if my scarf came up missing or if it got dirty or ripped or something."

"See. Now you trippin'. I told you I was gon' take care of it. I can trust you with my chain—my CHAIN—but you can't trust me with your scarf?"

Sa'Tahn loosened his grip on Alahna's hand a little. He looked to his left at the empty parking lot. Then he looked back at Alahna. He paused for a second, and then he said, "And it's just a scarf."

Alahna's eyes had been on the ground the whole time he was talking and he was still holding on to her hand with the chain in it. She had too much running through her mind to look at him, and she didn't want the tears to fall that had been forming in the rims of her eyes. But when he said "just a scarf" it was like a fire lit on the inside of her. She went from feeling fearful that something would happen...she went from feeling disappointed in herself for not honoring her mother's design and plan for her scarf...she went from feeling sad that the scarf might not ever be the same...and she went into RAGE! Before she knew it, her eyes were already instantly dried up. She felt her heart racing and the blood in her veins was heating up by the second. She yanked her hand from his hand and his chain hit the ground. She took one step back and said, "JUST A SCARF! JUST A SCARF????"

There was no way she could even get him to understand how special her scarf was. She didn't have time to tell him about her mother and their family tradition and where the material came from and what she was saving the scarf for. She definitely didn't want to go into that because she'd have to talk about how she took the scarf and used it outside of what it should have been used for. She was already hurt, and she was disappointed in herself that she was even in this predicament. All she could do was stand there and look at him. She couldn't believe that it was just a scarf to him. Why couldn't he just see how special it was to her because of the way she was protecting it? Why did she need to explain? Why couldn't he just understand that she didn't want him to take it with him and leave it at that?

He looked at her and busted out laughing. He said, "Girl, you tripppin'. If it gotta be all that, you can keep ya lil' scarf. Ain't nobody got time for you crying over no scarf. I don't need to hold nothin'. It's all good."

He bent over to get his chain off of the ground. Once he had it in his hand, he wiped it off one time, turned around, and walked off, leaving Alahna standing there alone. In a matter of seconds, her rage returned right back to hurt. The tears that had welled up and then dried up were coming uncontrollably now. She couldn't stop them if she tried.

All this time, Talia had been standing with a group of girls a little distance away from where Alahna and Sa'Tahn had been standing. She purposely left Sa'Tahn and Alahna alone so they could talk, but when Talia saw Sa'Tahn walk past her before his parents even arrived to pick him up, she knew something was wrong. She ran over to Alahna and saw her crying. She hugged her and asked her what was going on, but no matter what she said, and no matter what she did, Alahna wouldn't tell her what had happened.

By the time Alahna's mom got to the school to pick the girls up, Alahna had stopped crying as hard as she was when everything first happened, but she was still crying some, and she was still very obviously upset. When the girls got in the car, Alahna's mom thought it was strange that both of them got in the back seat, but she knew how inseparable the girls were and how they liked to talk ALL THE TIME about EVERYTHING. She decided not to pay it any real attention.

Alahna's mom asked, "Well how was it?"

Talia said, "It was fine."

"Just fine? That's it? You mean to tell me you girls didn't have the time of your lives after all of your preparations for months? Hmph…I thought sure you'd come in here and talk my ears off! Alahna, was it just 'fine' for you too?"

Alahna said, "Yea…"

There was a crack in her voice. She didn't sound like herself. Her mom looked in the rear view mirror to get a good look at her daughter, and she could see that Alahna had been crying. She immediately said, "What happened?"

She continued to drive and look at the road, then the rear view mirror…the road, then the rear view mirror.

Talia said, "I don't know, Mrs. Davenport. I tried to ask her what happened, but she wouldn't tell me."

Alahna began to cry again.

They were only about 3 minutes away from Talia's house. Alahna's mom wanted to stop right then, but she was close enough that she could get Talia home and try to get Alahna to talk once Talia had gotten out of the car.

"Baby, why are you crying?" Alahna's mom pleaded.

Alahna said nothing. She just kept crying. Her mom's heart broke! She hated not knowing what was wrong, but she hated, even more, not being able to take the pain away from her baby girl.

Alahna's mom pulled up to Talia's house. Talia thanked Mrs. Davenport for the ride and gave Alahna a hug. She walked up to her house, waited a bit for someone to open the door, and when someone finally opened the door, she waved to Mrs. Davenport as she walked in to let her know she was in okay.

Alahna's mom put the car in park, got out, and hopped in the back seat with Alahna. She grabbed Alahna and hugged her, and Alahna began to wail in her mother's arms. That always did it! If she was already upset and crying about something, and she would get a hug from her mom, the crying would get louder and stronger. She just about shuddered in her mom's arms in that backseat. She was a whirlwind of emotion.

Her mom just held her and said, "We can sit in this car all night if we have to. I can just hold you and let you cry forever. Don't say one word until you're ready."

She stroked Alahna's natural curls and rubbed her back. She squeezed her tight and rocked her gently. Her mom just wanted her to know that whatever it was, she could handle knowing it. She wanted her to know that she loved her and that she didn't have to be hurt all by herself. She didn't want to leave her in that moment of the obvious pain she was in. She wanted to comfort her.

Eventually, Alahna stopped crying and pulled back from her mom's embrace. She wiped what was left of her tears and stared down at her purse in her lap. Her mom just looked at her without saying a word. She wanted Alahna to speak whenever she was ready.

Alahna took a deep breath. She tried to look at her mom, but she couldn't. In all the while that she'd been crying, she honestly tried to think up something to tell her mom so she wouldn't have to tell her what really happened, but she couldn't think of anything big or bad enough to match how upset she was. No story would add up. Nothing she could think up could explain why she was THAT upset. Only the truth would explain the hurt she felt. Only the truth would explain why her tears were like a fountain.

She tried to look up again, but decided she'd just keep her head down and her eyes on her purse. She slowly reached into her purse and pulled out the case with her scarf in it. She sat it on top of her purse and closed her eyes.

There was silence.

About a minute later, she opened her eyes and looked at the case, and she saw two streaks of water rolling down the case. She was shocked, and thought for a second that she was crazy because she knew she wasn't crying anymore. How did the case get water on it, she thought. She looked up at her mom and saw that she was silently crying and looking at the scarf. Those were her mom's tears rolling down the case.

Alahna looked at her mom. She knew, instantly, that her mom was disappointed. She wanted to run and hide under a rock. She couldn't stand the thought of knowing she'd broken her mom's heart. Now Alahna was the one waiting in silence for her mom to speak.

When Mrs. Davenport opened her mouth to speak, she said, "So that's where it was."

Alahna looked up at her mom and her mouth flew open in disbelief. Her mom knew it was gone? How?

Her mom looked at her face of shock and answered all of the questions that were running through Alahna's mind. Alahna didn't have to ask. Her mom knew she was already embarrassed enough, so she did all the talking.

"Lahna, baby. I knew you took that scarf from your drawer. I knew it was gone when I went to put your laundry away. I thought maybe you'd moved it to another place in your room or something. I didn't think anything of it, honestly. I gave it to you and told you what it was for, but I left it with you. If you wanted to use it, you would, even if I told you not to. If you wanted to move it, it was yours to move. I hoped you would only use it for what it was intended, but again, you have your free will, and you make your own choices. I can teach you and tell you and guide you, but in the end, you decide."

Her mom wiped the tears from her eyes.

Her mom said, "I didn't know WHAT you did with it. I hoped it was just moved. So seeing it now has me feeling some different ways, and I'll be honest with you. I'm happy to see it because just knowing it was gone and not in its regular place was a little unnerving. But at the same time, I'm hurt because I just wanted you to honor what it was made for. I wanted you to use it for the reason it was created. And I took so much time with it. I used the finest fabric that I'll NEVER use EVER again for ANYONE else, and I used the perfect thread. I made it specifically with you in mind and wanted you to know how special it is not just to me, but FOR you."

"I know, Mom," Alahna whined. "That's why I was so upset. I used it with my outfit for the dance tonight and it was fine. I didn't dirty it and I didn't ruin it, but I was about to let Sa'Tahn keep it because he was going to let me keep his chain. And when I saw his hands touching it and when he kept asking me for it because he wanted something of mine to remember me by, he said it was 'just a scarf'. He said I was being too serious about it because I wouldn't let him keep it."

Alahna began to cry, but she talked through the tears.

"Mom, when he said that, I remembered what you said when you gave it to me, and I knew I broke your heart. I wasn't supposed to even take it out of the case."

Alahna sobbed and sobbed. Her mother hugged her.

"Alahna, I'm just happy to see it. And you don't even have to tell me you're sorry because 'sorry' was written all over you the moment you got in the car. It was written on every one of those tears. I can see that you know you messed up. What else can I or anyone else do? You're hurt enough for yourself, so I don't need to make it any worse."

She grabbed Alahna's chin and raised her face so she could look right into her eyes.

"Yes, you broke my heart, but you broke your own too. That lets me know that when I make this next one, it won't be used for anything but what it's created for. You don't want to hurt me anymore, and you don't want to feel this pain in your own heart anymore. That's certain."

Alahna couldn't believe what her mom had said! She was going to make another scarf?? But WHY? She had messed up the first one. It was supposed to be used to wipe her tears on her wedding day, but she didn't use it for that.

Her mom opened the case and took out the scarf. She wiped Alahna's tears until she stopped crying. When Alahna was calm, her mom put the scarf back in its case. She said, "We'll use this one for tonight's tears to remember them. We want to remember what made us cry in the first place so we'll never revisit anything like it again. It'll remind us of the purpose of the new scarf and that it should be used for nothing more than to wipe the tears on our wedding day."

Stories That Teach Girls

Alahna couldn't believe that her mom was saying and doing this! Was she in a dream? Had her mom really forgiven her? Wasn't she angry? Wasn't she scared that Alahna would mess it up again? How could she still love her and want to give her another gift after she messed that one up?

Her mom looked at her one last time and said, "Let's act like it never happened. We're gonna start over just like new, okay?" She kissed Alahna on her forehead and said, "I love you."

The White Scarf: Day 1 Study
ALAHNA AND THE WHITE SCARF

Before we jump into our study for today, let's first look at what a **metaphor** is. By definition, and in its simplest form, a **metaphor** is something used to represent something else. It's a symbol (dictionary.com). For example, If I was writing a poem to describe my mother's love for me, I could say, *"My mother's love is a warm blanket. When I'm cold, it wraps around me to take away the chill. And if I'm ill, it's the perfect companion. It snuggles me and removes all the pain I feel."*

Every time you read about the blanket in the poem, you should get a visual of my mother (a mother) in your mind. The blanket is a symbol for my mother. In your mind, you should see her arms around me and completely covering me like a blanket. That's what a good metaphor does. It causes you to see one thing as something else, and every time you see one thing in your mind, you see the other.

The White Scarf is one big metaphor. Everything in this story is a representation of, or a symbol for something else. This week we will dissect every symbol to better understand what God is saying to us through the story, and we're going to start with Alahna.

Alahna symbolizes YOU.

Yup. You heard me right. Alahna represents YOU.

She may be the past you. She may be the present you. She may even be the future you, but she's you. Every time she is mentioned in the story, it's you. Every time she does something, it's really you doing it. Every time she says something, it's really you saying it. You are Alahna. You're a fashionista with a big heart, a loving family and a really good best friend. You have a joy for life and you happen to have a little crush. ***insert heart eyes emoji*** And just like any girl who's ever had a crush, you want that crush to notice you, and give you a little attention. When that crush gives you that attention, it's exciting and warm and fuzzy and all is well with you. What happens, though, when all the excitement and warm and fuzzy feelings cloud your judgment and cause you to make decisions that you wish you could take back? What happens when you forget about promises you made with yourself and your family and God, and you do something to break those promises?

We'll examine that today, but we need to look at one more metaphor before we can dig in.

The white scarf is your body. Every time the white scarf is mentioned in the story, it symbolizes your body. Got it?

Okay. Let's dig in.

We've already studied this passage of scripture in another lesson, but it won't hurt to visit it again.

Read Psalm 139:13-16.

Verse 14 (NIV) says that you are _____ and

_____ made, which means everything about you is exactly the

way God wanted it to be.

Verse 16 (NIV) says that He saw your unformed body. You weren't even formed yet, but He still knew everything about you. That means He knew you **BEFORE** you even came to be. He knew you before even your mother did! **Verse 13 (NIV)** says that He knit you together in your mother's womb. He carefully put you together—every bone, every organ, every physical feature and personality trait, every gift, talent and ability—He knit it all together. Your body is His creation! He was careful in shaping your nose the way he wanted it and in giving you just the right skin tone. He gave your hair the texture He wanted it to have, and then He made sure to give you that smile of yours. He was very intentional in creating you. And then, because He took such great care in creating you and giving you your specific gifts, making you just the way He wanted you, He set you apart.

Read 1 Corinthians 6:19-20. Write it below.

_____

_____

God's word says that your body is a temple of the Holy Spirit who is **IN** you. That means, if you are a Christian and you've given your heart to Jesus and professed Him to be your savior and your Lord, your body is His dwelling place. He lives in your heart. Your heart is His home. You are the temple where He resides. This is why the scripture goes on to say that you are not your own and to honor God with your body because **YOUR BODY BELONGS TO HIM.**

Now, let's back up for just a second. Let's look at why God uses this metaphor, comparing our bodies to a temple. He could've called our bodies anything. He could've said our bodies are diamonds. He could've said our bodies are precious oils. Instead, He calls them temples. A temple is what He uses as a symbol for our bodies. Why?

Back in bible days, the time when this was written, the temple was considered THE holy place. The people of that day believed that the temple was *THE* place to honor God. It was the place where offerings were made to God. It was the place where prayers were spoken to God. It was God's place and it was respected as such. It was sacred and set apart. Not just anyone could enter the temple, and not just any activity could happen in the temple. Nothing was more sacred than the temple at that time. Years went into building one because every part of the temple was carefully planned out and designed with magnificent grandeur.

Only the finest materials were used when building the temple because it was designed to honor God. Most of the wood and fixtures for the chambers inside the temple were brought in from other cities to ensure that the materials were the best of the best. Thousands of men (30,000 men for the temple Solomon had built), and particularly skilled craftsmen and artists, worked tirelessly, year after year, to make the temple a place that they believed would please God. It HAD TO display splendor! It had to be majestic. It had to appear to be a holy place, and holier than any other place in the land.

Read 1 Kings 6:1-10.

Do you see the detail that went into building the temple? Can you imagine how long it must've taken to develop the plans and the designs for it? And did you see the word cubit when you read? A cubit is an ancient unit of measurement that measures the length of the forearm from elbow to middle finger tip, which is anywhere from 17 to 21 inches. If a cubit was the full projected 21 inches, and the width of the temple was 20 cubits, which is 420 inches, and if there are 12 inches in a foot, that means the width of the temple was 35 feet! The length was 105 feet (60 cubits, 1260 inches), and the height was 52 ½ feet (30 cubits, 630 inches). This temple was GRAND!

Read 1 Kings 6:14-22. What was laid over the inner sanctuary of the temple? Write it in all capital letters below.

_____

There was nothing cheap or "regular" used in the temple. Only the best of the best was used to complete the inside. PURE GOLD was laid over the inner sanctuary! And God, knowing all of this about a temple, decided to call your body a temple when he could have called it anything else. Wow! This says that, in God's eyes, your body is sacred and set apart, carefully thought out and constructed (created) with the finest materials. The outside of your temple is grand, but the inside, right at the heart of your temple is where the treasure has been laid. The outside of you doesn't even compare to who you are on the inside.

Stories THAT TEACH Girls

Now, remember that the white cloth is your body, and your body is a temple. How is the white cloth like the temple that's described in I Kings 6? Explain.

_____

_____

_____

The scarf was made of the best! The fabric was a pure white that Alahna's mom had never used on anyone before, just like the pure gold in the temple. The pearls on the scarf came from the coasts of Africa, just like the cedar (the finest wood) used for the temple came from Lebanon (I Kings 5:6-9). The scarf had beautiful silver threading, and all of the fixtures and decorative items that were placed in the inner sanctuary of the temple were special and extravagant like that thread. Your scarf...your temple...your body was specially crafted to be used for a specific purpose. Not just anything happens in a temple, and the scarf wasn't supposed to be used for just anything. It had a specific purpose. Your body isn't supposed to be used for just anything. It, too, is reserved for specific purposes at specific, appointed times.

Why do you think Alahna's mother went to such great lengths to make the scarf the way she did? Explain.

The White Scarf

_____

_____

_____

    She wanted it to be special for Alahna because Alahna was special to her. She wanted Alahna to have something no one else had because she wasn't like anyone else. She gave Alahns'a scarf a specific purpose because it wasn't just any scarf; it was special and set apart.

What was the purpose of Alahna's scarf?

_____

What did she use it for?

_____

What happened in Alahna's heart and mind when Sa'Tahn said, *"It's just a scarf"*?

_____

Thankfully, Alahna realized that her scarf shouldn't be used for anything other than what it was created for. Thankfully, she was reminded of just how special her scarf was. And YOU need to know, like Alahna, and like her scarf, YOU are special. YOU are set apart. YOU were masterfully crafted ON purpose with a purpose. You are not "just a girl" and you shouldn't treat yourself as such, and you certainly shouldn't allow anyone else to treat you like you're "just a girl". You are God's masterpiece, a grand temple, and you should ALWAYS present yourself that way!

The White Scarf: Day 2 Study
ALAHNA'S MOTHER, GWENDOLYN OLIVIA DAVENPORT (G.O.D.)

Think back to yesterday's lesson. In your own words, explain what a metaphor is.

_____

_____

_____

_____

To connect the metaphor, draw a line from a word in the left column to its corresponding word in the right column.

me   a temple

my body   Alahna

my body   the white scarf

Stories THAT TEACH Girls

Like we learned yesterday, if its' a good metaphor, every time you see one word, it's just like you're seeing the other. Let's take a look at another metaphor from the story:

Alahna's mom is God. Every time you see Alahna's mom in the story, you should think about God. Everything she says is what God is saying, and everything she does is what God is doing.

What was Alahna's mother's full name?

_____

So what are her initials?

_____

She has a name that forms those initials because in this story, she exemplifies God's characteristics.

Alahna's Mom Created (for) Her   (God Created You)

Psalm 139 reminds us that we were created in our mother's womb. God knit our bodies together. He is our Maker. Just like God did with our bodies, Alahna's mom knit the scarf together. She is the maker of the scarf. God took great care in making sure our features were exactly how He wanted them. We were made with precise intention, just like the temples were. And our bodies are temples. The temples were made with the finest materials that weren't used in any other buildings or dwellings. Alahna's mom did the same with the scarf. She made it with precise intention, using only the finest materials.

Alahna's Mom Wanted the Best for Her (God Wants the Best for You)

Alahns'a mom wanted the best for her, just like God wants for you. She went to great lengths to make sure Alahna had the best, and God does the same for you.

Read Psalm 103: 1-5. Write verse 5 below.

_____

_____

In this passage of scripture, the Lord is being praised for His goodness, and for the benefits we get from simply being His. He heals our diseases and he saves us from the pit and He satisfies our desires with GOOD things so our youth is renewed like the eagle (verse 5).

Have you ever been expecting something that you really wanted and when you went to look for it or you went to receive it, it wasn't what you hoped for? Yeah. I've had that happen too. It's quite a disappointment. It can really damper your mood. But I've also had times when I've been expecting something and when I went to get it or receive it, it was exactly what I wanted.

BOY, what a great feeling that was! This is what God means when He says our youth will be renewed like the eagle. When He fulfills our desires with His good things, He says it will excite us. It will give us the same type of excitement we feel when we receive things that we desire. He wants to give us that. He wants to satisfy us, not harm us. He wants the very best for us.

The story doesn't tell us how Alahna reacted when her mother presented her with the scarf at her 13th birthday party. All we know is that Alahna was aware of the family tradition. She knew that every girl in the family got something special from her mother to be used or given only at the time of her marriage. So Alahna had an expectation. She knew she would get something that she was supposed to treasure.

How do you think Alahna reacted when her mother presented her with the scarf and case and told her what it was for?

_____

_____

Proverbs 10:22 (KJV) says, *"The blessing of the Lord, it maketh rich, and he addeth no sorrow with it."*

I love this verse. Every time I read it, I'm reminded that whenever the Lord blesses me with good things, those good things are given to me to do just that—bless me. They're not given to me to bring me hurt, pain or sorrow. He doesn't bless me with any good thing with hopes of it bringing me sorrow. When Alahna's mom presented her with her scarf, her only vision was for

Alahna to wipe her tears of joy on her wedding day. She never even imagined anything else—it was created for that purpose. There shouldn't have been any sorrow connected to that scarf, but because Alahna didn't use the scarf the way it was designed to be used, **SHE** added sorrow to what was supposed to be her blessing. Her mom didn't give it to her with any sorrow attached. When we do with our scarves (bodies) what God tells us NOT to do, **WE** add sorrow. We hurt ourselves and bring ourselves pain. God was clear in saying that he adds no sorrow to the good things he gives us. If we experience sorrow with any of the blessings God gives us, we can always trace it back to where **WE** messed it up.

Alahna's Mom Already Knew (God Knows All Things)

How many times have you done something, thinking you got away with it, only to have your mom bust you out? I can't even count the number of times my mom called me out for something I thought was hidden. She knows me. She knew the kind of things I would do, and if something looked suspicious, based on what it was, my mom knew which of her 3 children did it. Alahna's mother, like any other mother, is the same way. She knows what's going on with her children and she knows what's going on in her house. That's how she knew that the scarf was gone.

Read Hebrews 4: 13. Write it on the next page.

Stories THAT TEACH Girls

_____

_____

God knows all things. There is NOTHING in creation that's hidden from His sight, especially you. He created you. He knows everything about you. He knows your thoughts and the very intent of your heart. The verse says that everything is laid bare before His eyes. In other words, He sees through anything you try to fake and anything you try to hide. He knows the you that no one else knows. You don't even know the you that He knows. You may be able to fool other people, but there's no fooling God.

Read Psalm 139:7-8. Summarize these scriptures below.

_____

_____

There is no running from God. Wherever you go, He's there.

Alahna's Mom Gives Comfort/Shows Compassion (God Wants to Give You Comfort and Compassion)

Alahna messed up. Her mother could have flipped out, but she loved Alahna too much to make her pain any worse. In fact, when she saw that her daughter was upset, it hurt her too much for her to even be angry. All she wanted to do was comfort her.

Believe it or not, our parents hurt when we hurt, even if we cause our own pain when they told us not to do that very thing that caused us the pain. It's the nature of love. Love loves even when we think it shouldn't love. And that's definitely God's love. That's His comfort too. Even when we cause ourselves pain, He comes to us to comfort us and love us.

Read Isaiah 66:13. Write it below.

_____

_____

In this chapter, God is actually talking to a city full of people who were doing their own thing. Everything He said to do, they did the exact opposite. And it wasn't the first time! But He had mercy on them. There were some who messed up, but wanted to do the right thing, and God told them that He would take care of them and comfort them. I can imagine, when God pointed out their wrong, like Alahna's mom did, they were hurt because they realized they'd broken His heart. He let them know that He wasn't pleased, but He still comforted them, just like Alahna's mom did with her when Alahna broke her heart.

God will always love us; His love doesn't end. When we mess up, it's the love He has for us that causes Him to comfort us and have compassion on us. Especially when He sees that we are genuinely sorry. When He sees that we have Godly sorrow, He doesn't mind extending His comfort and compassion.

Alahna's Mom Let Her Start Fresh (God Lets You Start Fresh)

2 Corinthians 7:10a (NIV) says, *"Godly sorrow brings repentance that leads to salvation and leaves no regret…"*

Having Godly sorrow is very different from simply saying "I'm sorry" or "I apologize" for something you did. Take Tiffany for example. Tiffany accidentally stepped on Jessica's shoe when she had to step over her to get to her seat. Tiffany didn't say "Excuse me" or "I'm sorry" because she felt like Jessica's foot was in the way and shouldn't have been in the aisle. Tiffany felt like Jessica should've moved her foot when she saw her walking by.

Jessica was hurt that Tiffany stepped on her shoe and didn't apologize. There was a little dirt on Jessica's shoe, so she asked her teacher if she could step out to clean it really quickly. Her teacher asked how her shoe got dirty when she was doing nothing but sitting in her seat. Jessica told her that Tiffany stepped on it when she was walking past her to get to her seat. The teacher could see that Jessica was a little upset, so she asked if Tiffany had apologized to her. Jessica said she hadn't. The teacher called Tiffany up and told her to apologize to Jessica, and Tiffany apologized, but only because the teacher told her to, not because she really wanted to.

Tiffany's example is not the same as me accidentally stepping on a girl's shoe and immediately apologizing because I sincerely didn't mean to do it. Tiffany's example is not like me offering to walk with the girl to the restroom so I can clean the dirt off of her shoe because I was the one to put it there. Tiffany's example is not like me giving the girl a hug and looking her in the eye and apologizing one last time before we walk out of the restroom together. It hurt my heart to see her upset about her shoe, especially since I was the one to cause the hurt. That's Godly sorrow. Tiffany's example was not.

Alahna knew she had broken her mother's heart, and it was evident that that was the last thing she ever wanted to do. I mean, she was more upset that she hurt her mother than she was about anything Sa'Tahn said or did. Her own situation wasn't even that important when she realized she may have hurt her mom. She had Godly sorrow—she was so hurt by her own doing that she was determined to never even revisit that type of incident again. And Alahna's mother gave her the opportunity to start over with a new scarf for that very reason. She knew, because of that Godly sorrow, Alahna would use the new scarf the way that it was intended to be used. There was no question about that. Like 2 Corinthians 7:10a says, her Godly sorrow brought repentance—she turned from her wrong and walked toward what was right.

Read 1 John 1:9. Write it below.

_____

_____

God does for us exactly what Alahna's mom did for her. When we have Godly sorrow for something we did and confess that to Him, He forgives us, and cleanses us from all unrighteousness. We get to start over, just like getting a fresh new white scarf. Alahna's mom took the old scarf and dried Alahna's tears, and that became the scarf for her to always remember what caused her sorrow. That scarf reminded her to never revisit a situation like that again. The new scarf would be a reminder of her mother's love for her. It would be a reminder of her compassion for her. It would be a reminder to Alahna that being allowed to start over is truly a blessing.

   If your scarf has been compromised or if you've chosen to do something with it that it wasn't designed to do, the creator of the scarf, when He sees your genuine Godly sorrow and knows that in your heart you deeply desire not to mess it up again, He is willing to make you a new one. And if you have, you're not the only girl. Trust me. I never let anyone have my scarf, but I'll tell you, I wanted to let someone have it, and I almost did. I was Alahna. I took my scarf out of its case. I let someone get real close to it. I thought for a second about letting him hold on to it for a time, but then, just like Alahna, something snapped me back into reality. I realized that my scarf was created for a specific purpose and time. And just like Alahna's mom did for her, God did the same for me. He let me have a new one. And like Alahna, I was hurt that I didn't keep my scarf in its case, safely tucked away in my drawer. I was hurt that I took it out and almost used it for something other than what it should be used for. And I was hurt because I knew I hurt the One who created my scarf. It was almost like I could feel His tears. But He comforted me and showed me in His word, like I just showed you, that He could cleanse me from all unrighteousness. He could let me start over, and I'm so glad He did! I have a whole new scarf that's waiting to be used on my wedding day because the One who made it says that's the appointed time.

The White Scarf

What is the Lord saying to your heart right now after doing today's study? Pour it all out below.

_____

_____

_____

_____

_____

_____

_____

_____

_____

_____

Stories THAT TEACH *Girls*

The White Scarf: Day 3 Study

SA'TAHN

Today, let's look more closely at Sa'Tahn. He, too, like everyone else in this story, is a metaphor.

Sa'Tahn is Satan himself. He is the enemy. He is the adversary whose ultimate goal is to destroy us. Every time Sa'Tahn says something in the story, it's really Satan saying it. Any time Sa'Tahn does anything in the story, it's really Satan doing it.

Read John 10:10. Why did Jesus come?

_____

_____

Why does the enemy (Satan) come?

_____

_____

Jesus wants us to have abundant (full, prosperous, joyous) life. That's why He died for us. He died so our sins could be covered which gives us right standing with God. He literally gave His life so we could have life. But the enemy comes to **1) Kill 2) Steal** and **3) Destroy**. That's it. No other reason.

You can bank on it. When the enemy presents himself in your life, he is looking to destroy you in some way. Sa'Tahn could've asked Alahna for anything of hers that night at the school dance. He mentioned her ring; he could've focused on that. He could've asked for her earrings or her bracelets. He could've even taken a picture of her with his phone if he really wanted something to remember her by, but why didn't he? I mean, let's think about it. Why was he so interested in a belt *(what he called it)* anyway? What was he planning to do with it? What *could* he do with it? Why was he *that* driven to have a girl's belt? What boy do you know goes around asking girls, *"Hey, can I hold on to your belt until tomorrow?"* Really? Why her belt? I could see a boy asking to hold on to a girl's jacket or something else that makes even a little sense like a cap if she were wearing one, but a belt? A belt that I'm sure doesn't fit him because boys' and girls' waists are different and girls' and boys' belts are made differently.

And on top of that, he barely knew her. They only looked at each other in the halls at school. That night at the dance was their first time talking. Why, oh WHY, would he even ask for the personal belongings of someone he doesn't even know? You want to know why?

Because it's the enemy's job to take whatever he can from us!

And he wants the things that matter the most to us because losing what's important to us can **steal** our joy, **kill** our peace, and **destroy** our hope.

Let me give you an example. Marriage is God's idea; He created marriage. When people join together in marriage, it brings glory to God, and because God loves it, the enemy (Satan) hates it! He can't stand to see marriages doing well, and He wants to destroy anything that brings glory to God, so he sends all kinds of distractions and cunning schemes to destroy marriages.

One couple, in particular, Ciara and Daryl, have been married for 5 years, but have been together for 8 years, since they were freshmen in college. They love everything about each other, and they love being married. People often tell them that their marriage is an example of what marriage is supposed to be like. They both work and have very busy schedules, but they set aside 2 days a week to have lunch and/or dinner together with their cell phones turned completely off. They make it a point to pull away from everything that's going on so they can focus on each other. They also mentor and counsel young college-age couples, and pray with them on a regular basis. They do double dates with those couples every now and then too. Ciara and Daryl are each other's best friend, and they want other couples to get along that same way.

One day, Ciara was leaving a lunch meeting with some of her colleagues, and when she walked outside of the restaurant, she saw Daryl standing in front of a department store a little further down and across the street, laughing and talking with another woman. His hand was on her shoulder as they talked, and it looked a lot more friendly to Ciara than she had ever seen her husband with any woman. She couldn't believe her eyes, so she walked a few steps forward so she could see a little better, and sure enough, it was Daryl. Ciara was furious!

Even though she knew in her heart that Daryl would not dishonor her or their marriage that way, she couldn't help but focus on what she saw with her own two eyes. The more she thought about it, the more upset she became. She wanted to not think about it, but it was ALL she thought about for the rest of her workday.

Instead of going on their dinner date later that evening, Ciara told Daryl by text message that she had to cancel because her boss needed her to work on some important documents for the next day. She had never canceled before, so Daryl thought it must be real important. He said he would see her later and since they were having dinner in different places, they could have dessert together at home. She agreed, but she had no intention of having dessert with him. She was too upset.

Ciara lied about having to work late so she could call her friends and meet them for dinner instead. She told them what happened and they flipped out! These were friends she had known since college, who walked in her wedding as bridesmaids and knew the nature of Ciara's relationship with Daryl. Even THEY knew that he would never dishonor Ciara in that way, but it didn't stop them from adding fuel to the fire that was already blazing within her. When they should have been encouraging Ciara to talk about it with Daryl, they did the exact opposite. One friend said, *"Girl, I would have been waiting at home for him with a knife in my hand requesting some answers."* The other friend said, *"Don't go home. Make him feel it. If he gon' be talking to other women, let's see how it feels when he don't have HIS woman to talk to."*

Ciara realized at that very moment that she needed to be talking this through with her husband. She was getting advice to do things that she would never do, and she actually considered it for a moment. She knew a great hotel she could go to, but that wasn't what she and Daryl decided to do in their marriage. How could she NOT go home? When they first got engaged and prayed together about how they were going to handle conflict in their marriage, they agreed that they would talk about everything, no matter how difficult. They would never sleep away from each other because they knew it was best to work things out and not run from them. They even counseled other couples on talking about their issues immediately and not running from them. They had seen too many examples in other marriages where husbands and wives didn't talk about things and their situations only got worse. Ciara and Daryl learned to deal with things head on, and this was one of the times when they needed it most.

    Ciara got in her car to head home and she cried the whole way there. She couldn't believe she let her anger keep her from at least asking her husband who the woman was or what caused them to be standing together outside of that store. And to get so angry that she called friends to let them know what's going on in her very personal relationship with her husband... So not like her! The advice they gave was against EVERYTHING she and her husband ever agreed on, and it was a good thing she went home to talk to her husband about everything. After talking to Daryl, she found that she was WAY off! The woman that Daryl was talking to was his brother's ex-girlfriend from college, who happened to be a woman that Ciara knew too. They had classes together in college and even hung out a few times. Daryl and the woman had seen each other in the store while Daryl was picking up a "Just Because" gift for Ciara. They were talking about old times and catching up with one another so much that they talked right on out the store together. What Ciars saw was the end of their conversation and Daryl wishing her well as he said good-bye.

The enemy had caused Ciara to see something that really wasn't there. And THAT'S what he does. He is SO cunning! He is sly. He will make suggestions to have us think that a situation is more than it really is, like he did with Ciara. He will cause us to get upset over nothing so we can have arguments and be in strife with others. And he especially wanted that with Ciara and Daryl because their marriage pleased God. Even worse than Ciara's own thoughts were the suggestions the enemy gave her through her friends. Have a knife in her hand? Don't go home when she and her husband vowed that they'd never do that? DEFINITELY THE ENEMY! Every thought or suggestion that Ciara had was to do something that would not please God or that would not honor her marriage. That was a sure sign that the enemy was at work trying to **steal** her joy, **kill** her marriage, and **destroy** her peace.

And the enemy is no different with us. Do you hear me? **HE'S NO DIFFERENT!** How many times have you been upset about something to later learn that there really wasn't anything to be upset about? How many times have you discovered that if you just would have waited a little bit to hear a situation out, or if you would have talked to a person to get the truth, the issue really wasn't an issue at all? What happens is sometimes "problems" look like problems, and they're really not problems at all. If we don't take time to analyze the situation and see it for what it really is, we can really cause ourselves (and others) some unnecessary pain and drama.

The enemy was trying to get Ciara to do something that would only end up hurting her even more. Daryl would have been hurt that Ciara didn't talk to him, and he probably would've gotten angry because she ignored their agreement to talk about everything. That would have started a cycle of hurt and mistrust in their marriage that could have probably ended in divorce if it went on long enough. And that's what the enemy wants. He starts where he can. He looks for any open window to start working on taking what's dear to us. Ciara and Daryl loved each other. They loved their marriage. The enemy took a small opportunity to try and maximize a little NOTHING into a BIG something. Ciara was about to **kill** her marriage. The enemy was digging his heels in so he could **steal** her peace of mind, and he was looking to **destroy** their ability to fix their small issue that wasn't really even an issue at all. That's what he does, and that's what Sa'Tahn did with Alahna.

Sa'Tahn was trying his best to find a way to get something from Alahna, and it wasn't even about the scarf. It was simply about seeing if he could take something that mattered to her, away from her. It was nothing but an attempted conquest for him. When he saw that the scarf was meaningful to Alahna, he locked in on it, and when he locked in on it, he kept at it. After setting his sights on the scarf, he wasn't concerned about anything else. In fact, his persistence only intensified when he saw that Alahna wasn't letting go of the scarf so easily. He wanted to **steal** her ability to think clearly, so he used fluffy words. He was charming. He flashed his smile here and there, and he even began to whisper to her. He used his smooth talk to try and convince Alahna that he would take good care of the scarf. He pleaded and pleaded with her, telling her that it would be okay in his care. Then he said he would give her something of his own that he considered special because He thought she would be more willing to give him something special of hers. His plan was to TAKE, and that's it! If she would've given him the scarf, she would've given him her peace. Shoot...she didn't even give him the scarf and her peace was destroyed, so just think if she *did* actually give it to him!

Then, just like Satan does, Sa'Tahn throws a fit when he can't have it his way. Satan throws a fit when we choose God over Him. He's mad when his tactics don't work. When Alahna didn't give Sa'Tahn that scarf, he started hurling insults and treating her like trash. He got so mad that it didn't go his way that he walked away and didn't want to have anything to do with her anymore, and that was a sign. It was a sign that he never wanted HER in the first place. He didn't want to be with Alahna. He only wanted what Alahna could give him. He was selfish! All he cared about was himself! Do you remember what James 3 says about selfish ambition? Where there's selfishness, you'll find disorder and every evil practice. *(If someone who is "interested" in you is only out for themselves, BEWARE!)*

Read Genesis 2:15-17 and Genesis 3.

You see? Satan is persistent in his pursuit to get you to turn away from what you know is right. He will keep pressing and pressing. In Genesis 3, Eve knew exactly what the Lord had said. She even repeated it to Satan in verse 2. She said, *"We may eat from the trees in the garden, but God did say, 'You must not eat fruit from the tree that is in the middle of the garden, and you must not touch it, or you will die.'"* And then, Satan, with all of his craftiness said, and I paraphrase, *"C'mon Eve. Did God REALLY say not to eat from that tree? Are you sure you heard him right? Cuz, see, I've eaten from the tree, and I'm alright. He just knows if you eat from the tree, you'll be wise like Him, and he don't want that. He don't want you to know what He knows because He wants it all to himself. Why would He give you all of these trees in the garden and then tell you not to each from just that one? I mean, come ooooon, Eve. Girl, eat from that tree. You will not surely die."*

Eve fell for the crafty words. She fell for the smooth talk. She gave in to his persistence, and she even gave the fruit to her husband. As soon as they ate fruit from the tree, they learned why God didn't want them to, but it was too late. They had already disobeyed God, and the enemy had won in his conquest. *(This is when sin officially entered the world.)*

Alahna was SO hurt because what was sacred to her meant nothing to Sa'Tahn. He *acted* like the scarf was important enough for him to take care of, but the moment she didn't want to give it to him, he showed his true colors. When someone cares about you and they see that something hurts you or bothers you or makes you feel uncomfortable, they don't push. And if they become angry, they're selfish. They want what they want. They don't care about you. Be mindful of that type of behavior because just like God's spirit can live inside of us and cause us to do what's right, Satan's spirit can work through people and make them do wrong.

After today's study, if you come across "a Sa'Tahn," you should know it, and as soon as you know it, RUN! Run in the opposite direction!

What did you learn today about Satan and how he operates?

_____

_____

_____

_____

The White Scarf: Day 4
THE PROVERBS STUDY

    Without a doubt, the best part of Alahna's situation was her mother's forgiveness. Alahna's mother wasn't exactly pleased that she had used her scarf before her wedding day, but she was quick to forgive her and show her love. Gwen was pleased that Alahna confessed. She was pleased that Alahna saw for herself how damaging it is to break a personal vow. Alahna felt so much pain for her own actions that she didn't even need a punishment from her mother. She was suffering enough within herself from her choice; she knew she had messed up.

    Alahna's mother gave her grace. She wiped Alahna's slate clean and let her start over like nothing ever happened. She made Alahna a brand new scarf and told her to see the old scarf only as a reminder of what *not* to do. She told her that the new scarf would wipe the tears of joy, but the old scarf would hold the tears of pain, and that those tears of pain were tears she never needed to revisit. What a shame it would be if Alahna decided to treat the new scarf like she treated the old one! What a waste and dishonor of her mother's grace and forgiveness!

Read Proverbs 26:11. Write it in the space below in ALL CAPS.

_____

Can you imagine being sick with a stomach virus and vomiting all over the floor, and then just a few minutes after you release your vomit, you go back to it to eat some of it? Ewwwwww, right? The most disgusting thing EVER! But the Lord says when we go back to our "trash," we're no different from a dog going back to its vomit.

And what is our "trash"? Our "trash" is anything we let go of or get rid of that we KNOW is no good for us. For example, the doctor told Kia that she should COMPLETELY stay away from fried foods because of how it affects the lining of her stomach and how it causes her excruciating pain. She stays away for 3 months, but then she breaks down at a party and eats fried chicken. From that day forward, she eats fried foods at least twice a week. Before long, she's back at the doctor's office in pain, and finds out that her situation is worse than it was before.

The bible calls Kia a fool! She knew what wasn't good for her. She got rid of it for a while, but she returned to it, only to have more severe consequences than she had the first time. We do this too. We knew the girls we were hanging with were trouble. When we got in trouble with them, we decided not to be in their company. For a long time, we didn't hang out with them, but one day, we decided to give them another try. It didn't take long to fall right back into the same trouble we were in with them the first time, and the bible calls us fools for going back to that "trash".

We know that boy is no good for us. We saw how he talked to other girls, but we still wanted his attention. When he talked to us that way, we realized that we were right about him all along. We kick him to the curb, and for a while, we pay him no attention, but one day he apologizes. He says he's not the same and he wants to show us that he's different, so we give in and decide to start talking to him again. It wasn't long before he went right back down that same, very familiar road of talking to us with no respect. He was a lot like Sa'Tahn too, because when things didn't go his way, he got angry which made him mean and caused him to handle us in a rough way, and WE KNEW THIS. The bible calls us fools for going back to that "trash".

Alahna would be a fool to go back and seek Sa'Tahn's attention. She already knows that he doesn't care about her or her scarf. She would be a fool to do with the new scarf what she did with the old one.

And there are so many other examples of "trash" that we could go back to. It could be music we let go of. It could be television shows that we know aren't pleasing to the Lord. It could be habits that we know aren't pleasing to the Lord. Anything we go back to that we KNOW isn't pleasing to the Lord and keeps us from being in close relationship with Him, is "trash", and the bible calls us fools for going back to it.

DON'T BE A FOOL!

The White Scarf: Day 5
CHALLENGE/ACTIVITY

Share What You've Learned

Your challenge today is to share this story, *The White Scarf*, with a friend. Use the time that you would normally do your study to share this story with someone else. You can read it to her, or you can summarize it and just tell her what happened. If you really trust her to read from your book *(at this point you have a lot of personal notes and thoughts in your book)*, then let her read it from your book, but she'll have to read it today and return it today because you have to do your study tomorrow. Since we're in the true technology age, you can even snap pictures of the pages and send them to her by text *(Make sure the page numbers are visible in the pictures)*.

Then, after she's read (or heard) the story, talk about it. Share with her what you've learned from God's word in this week's study about the story. Explain the metaphors in the story to her to help her understand. Then, talk to her about some of the things you've learned for yourself from God's word and give her an opportunity to talk about some things she learned about herself.

BONUS

Take one of your gifts and use it to discuss the story with your friend. For example, if I were a poet, I would write a poem to summarize the main idea of the story, and I'd share that with her. If I were an artist, I'd draw a little something from a scene or from an idea in the story and give it to her so she can always remember what she read. **THIS** is ministry. You've learned some things about God's love for us, and now you get to share it with someone else.

Stories THAT TEACH *Girls*

The White Scarf: Day 6
A WAY OF ESCAPE, GOD'S HOLY SPIRIT

Read 1 Corinthians 10:13. Write it below.

_____

_____

None of what you read in Alahna's story is uncommon. We will ALL, at some point, have someone we're interested in, and we will ALL have someone interested in us. We will have the option of doing the right thing or doing the wrong thing with them. It will be our choice. God always allows us to choose, and we can choose to honor Him or not, but one thing is for sure: **He always provides the opportunity for us to escape a wrong choice.** There is ALWAYS a way. Sure, I may have very well gotten myself into the situation that I need to escape, but God loves me so much that He *wants* me out. He will provide the way EVERY time, but I have to take it.

What word did Alahna hear Sa'Tahn say that snapped her back into reality?

_____

When Sa'Tahn said, *"You gon' be takin' care of me like that when we're **married**,"* Alahna snapped back into reality. He said **married** and she remembered that her scarf was supposed to be used on her wedding day—not before. **That moment was God's Holy Spirit.** That was the Holy Spirit's way of stepping in and providing Alahna's way of escape. She was about to give away her most prized possession, but the Lord intervened to give her a way out. Even though the enemy was right in the middle of his cunning schemes, trying to convince Alahna to give him her scarf, the Lord made sure she heard that one word to snap her back into reality. God loved her too much to not give her a way out. It was her choice to take it or leave it.

If you have accepted Jesus Christ as your Lord and Savior, God's Holy Spirit lives in you. He is your help and your guide. Listen for His ways out. Look for His ways out. His way of escape is always there when you're tempted to do something you shouldn't or when you, like Alahna, are in a situation where your head isn't clear because you're in the "love cloud", floating on air from all the attention you're getting from that special someone. And I'm not telling you something somebody told me. I'm telling you what I know. I'm a witness! I know that the Lord can cause the phone to ring right in the knick of time. I know that that phone call can be one that you HAVE TO answer because it's a matter of life or death on the other end. I know that that phone call could be the cause of you leaving a very tempting situation right when things are about to go to a place that you may think you want, but you know deep down you really don't. I know the Holy Spirit can do that, and I know that God loves you so much that He WILL provide those kinds of ways to keep you.

Have you ever heard someone say something like, *"I just have this feeling,"* or *"Something about this isn't right,"* or *"Something told me not to do that"*? Some people say that's their conscience talking. For those of us who are in Christ, that is the Lord's Holy Spirit talking. LET. HIM. PROTECT. YOU. Let Him. Take the way out! It's for your own good.

The White Scarf: Day 7
JOURNAL

Write a letter to yourself. The you of today is writing a letter to the older you who will open this letter on your wedding day. What do you want to say to yourself?

_____

_____

_____

_____

_____

_____

_____

Stories That Teach Girls

Family Ties, Part 1
by Iantha Ussin (Ms. I.)

Stories that Teach Girls

Karen and Will always knew they wanted three children. Even before they were married, they talked about the family they wanted to have. They didn't care if they had all boys or all girls or a mix. They just wanted three. Their first child was a boy. They named him Nathan. Two years later, they had a girl. They named her Natasha. Once Natasha turned a year old, Karen and Will started trying for their third child. They started lovingly preparing the nursery just as they had done with Nathan and Natasha. They cleaned out all the things they had used for Natasha that they knew they couldn't use for the new baby, and they held on to things that they knew they could. Will repainted the crib to make it like new. He built a new shelf to put into the room because they had learned over the years that babies need lots of storage for their "baby stuff," as Will called it. Karen and Will even decided to repaint the room a neutral yellow because this time, they wanted to be surprised with the sex of the baby. Karen wanted another boy. Will wanted another girl.

The nursery was perfect after they did everything they needed to do to make it like new. For about two months after the nursery had been completed, Karen and Will would visit it together every morning and pray for their unborn child. They asked the Lord to bless them with another healthy child that they could love and guide in His ways. Karen would always pray for a son, and Will would always pray for a daughter, and they would laugh because although they had their personal desires, they really both just wanted a healthy child to love.

Years passed. Natasha would be turning 5 years old in three months and Karen still wasn't pregnant. Karen was afraid that she might not be able to have another child because it was taking so long. She talked her concerns and anxieties over with Will. He prayed with her and reminded her not to fear. He reminded her that God's will would be done and that no matter what it was, they had to understand and trust that it was His best plan for them.

With tears in his eyes as he prayed with Karen one morning in the nursery, Will said, "We have to trust in the Lord and lean not to our own understanding. We have to continue to acknowledge Him in all our ways and know that He is directing our path. If He says 'not now' for our child, then we'll wait. But we have to trust that He knows what's best for us."

He hugged Karen tight like he always did after they prayed. That morning, he held on to her a little while longer to comfort her heavy heart. After that prayer with her husband, Karen settled it in her heart to just trust God's timing. He had already blessed them with two beautiful children who were intelligent and loving and talented and funny (Nathan was the family clown), and she believed that God would do it again. From that moment, she was determined to focus on Nathan and Natasha. She wanted to be the best mother she could be for them.

And Will was certainly *Dad of the Year*. He attended EVERY one of Natasha's gymnastics practices from the time she was 3 years old. When she turned 6 and began to compete on the pre-junior level, he would sit right beside her coach. He wanted to make sure Natasha saw him whenever she looked over at her coach for direction or instruction. She was the apple of her dad's eye. She was his baby girl. She was his Pinky Binky, the name he gave her as a baby because Karen dressed her in pink so much.

Nathan was an athlete too. Aside from being a master jokester, he was a pretty good basketball player. He started bouncing a basketball at the age of 4 and blew his parents' socks off! It was like he was born to do it. He had no problem handling the ball, and with a little practice with his dad on the patio in their back yard, he was dribbling skillfully by age 5. There was no doubt that he was going to be a skilled player, so his parents enrolled him in a local recreation team's biddy ball program.

He was team captain by his second season. He did nothing but excel every year after that.

Karen and Will were extremely busy with Nathan and Natasha and their practice schedules and meets and games. They were so involved with their children's lives that the thought of a third child was pushed to the back of their minds. Sure, they still wanted that child, and every now and then, they would remember to pray together about it, but they didn't pray nearly as often as they had before. They were seriously just trusting God's timing. It would happen when it would happen. And the year that Nathan turned 9 and Natasha turned 7, Karen and Will found out that Karen was finally pregnant with the third child they had prayed for and always wanted.

Everyone in the family was excited about the new baby, so the months seemed to fly by. It was like one day the family was shopping for cute baby clothes and other "baby stuff," and the next, they were rushing Karen to the hospital to deliver the baby that they couldn't wait to meet. Natasha was like her dad; she wanted a girl. Nathan was like his mom; he wanted a boy. But none of that mattered to anyone in the family when the beautiful, bright-eyed baby girl made her long-awaited entrance. They were instantly in love! Karen and Will decided to name her Natalie.

Natalie fit perfectly into their family. She was a calm baby, only crying if she was wet or dirty or if she was ready to eat. She laughed at all of Nathan's jokes whenever he acted a complete fool to get her attention, and Natasha loved having a little sister around that she could talk to about dolls and dress up, even if Natalie couldn't understand a word her big sister was saying. And Karen and Will loved Natalie more than she would ever know. There were times when Natasha and Nathan would both be away from home at a neighbor's house or at a church youth function, and Karen and Will would just snuggle on the couch with Natalie for hours. She brought so much love into their home.

Natalie was no different from her brother and sister with her gifts and talents either. It was right around age 4 when Karen and Will knew Natasha would excel in gymnastics. It was around age 4 when they knew Nathan would excel in basketball. Natalie was 4 when she took an interest in the piano. She could hardly sit still at church on Sundays when Ms. Weldon was playing, and it wasn't because she enjoyed the music so much. She definitely enjoyed it, but she was more interested in seeing what Ms. Weldon was doing to produce the sound that came from the piano. She was trying to figure out what her hands were doing, and if the sound was coming from what she was doing with her hands, why were her feet moving? Natalie would rush over to the piano at the end of service and hug Ms. Weldon and ask her to play. She would sit there and watch with undeniable interest, holding a fixed gaze on Ms. Weldon's hands. She would peer down at Ms. Weldon's feet every now and then, but only for a few seconds. Her eyes would quickly jump back up to Ms. Weldon's hands. After this happened every Sunday for about 2 months, Karen and Will decided to ask Ms. Weldon if she would be willing to give Natalie private lessons. They wanted to see if Natalie's natural interest in the piano had any real depth. Ms. Weldon gladly took Natalie on as her first 4-yr-old student, and within months, Natalie was showing signs of being a promising pianist. She was a natural! It was evident why her interest was so strong; she was made to play the piano. Her family would soon learn that she was born to play many other instruments too.

By the age of 8, Natalie had completely fallen in love with making music. When Ms. Weldon introduced her to wind instruments, she took a liking to the clarinet. When she was introduced to brass instruments, it was the saxophone because it was like the clarinet in so many ways. But it was when she was introduced to string instruments that she REALLY fell in love. The violin captured Natalie's heart even more than the piano had, and it would be the violin that would be her greatest treasure. After seeing Natalie's progress with all of her instruments, but especially the piano and violin, Ms. Weldon talked to Karen and Will about having Natalie attend Brimmington School of the Arts (BSA) where she could begin to play all genres of music and learn everything else there was to know about music from some of the best musicians and music teachers in the country. Without even taking any real time to discuss it, Karen and Will knew that that was where Natalie should be. Music was her passion and all she ever talked about. Nothing made her happier. Any extra time she had, she spent that time playing music or watching pianists and violinists on YouTube. Enrolling her in BSA was a no brainer. And so, at the age of 9, Natalie began her journey in music at BSA, and what a journey it would be! The whole family was about to experience what it was like to be a student at BSA.

Students in Kindergarten through 3rd grade did not participate in school shows or outside school-sponsored performances. They weren't allowed to participate until 4th grade, so Natalie started attending the school right in time to be involved in school shows, and because she was so skilled, she was landing spots in show after show. Her family was super excited about the opportunity for her, but that was before they knew how much it would require of them all.

As time passed, and there were more and more rehearsals and performances and weekend trips, Karen and Will were having a hard time juggling all of the kids' schedules. Natalie's, alone, was a lot to handle. What started happening, unfortunately, was one parent had to be with Natalie because she had the most demanding schedule of all three children, and one parent had to split time between Natasha's and Nathan's events. There were times when neither parent was at Natasha's gymnastics practices or meets because one was with Natalie and one was with Nathan, and there were times that no parent was with Nathan because one parent was with Natasha, and one was with Natalie. Of all the years that Nathan and Natasha had been involved in sports, they had NEVER had a parent miss a game or meet, and it hurt. They understood what was going on, and they knew their parents were doing the best they could, but it still hurt.

On the evening of one of Natalie's school shows when Natasha didn't have any gymnastics practice, one parent was supposed to go to Natalie's show, and one parent was supposed to take Natasha to see Nathan play in a district basketball game. There was some miscommunication between Karen and Will and both parents showed up at Natalie's show. Because they didn't go together, they didn't sit together. Neither parent even knew that the other was there! Natasha had been at a neighbor's house waiting to be picked up to head to Nathan's game. When the waiting got a little long, Natasha finally called her dad, who then called her mom, and they finally realized that they were both at the show. By the time Will left Natalie's show, swooped by the house to get Natasha, and drove across town to see Nathan, the game was in the 4th quarter.

Nathan had played pretty much all of the first 3 quarters, and his team was up by 30 points, so Nathan's coach let him rest on the bench for the 4th quarter. His dad didn't even see him play. Nathan was hurt. He was frustrated. He was tired of taking a back seat to Natalie and all of her school events. He missed the way the family had been before Natalie started school at BSA.

Natasha was feeling it too, especially since she was her daddy's girl. She had grown accustomed to seeing her dad at her gymnastics meets because he never missed. The first meet he missed because of one of Natalie's weekend concerts, Natasha could hardly focus. She kept looking into the crowd to see if he'd shown up, but every time she looked, he wasn't there. She went into the locker room after that meet and cried. When her dad showed up later to pick her up so they could meet the rest of the family for dinner, she was extremely quiet. She didn't have much to say at all. Her dad asked questions, but he got one word answers from her. He just thought she had a bad meet like she sometimes did, and he'd learned over the years not to push or ask too many questions because it only made her more upset. He learned that she would talk when she was ready. This time, though, she actually wanted him to ask more questions. She wished he would comfort her. She wished he could see that her heart wasn't broken over the meet, but that it was broken because she missed her daddy. She wished he wouldn't apologize for missing her meet because of Natalie's concert. She was tired of hearing about how she was missing out because Natalie needed him. Why couldn't he miss some of Natalie's stuff? Why couldn't one parent be at one of Natasha's events and one parent at one of Nathan's and somebody miss one of Natalie's for a change? Nathan and Natasha were older and a bit more independent, but it didn't mean that they didn't still need their parents' support. Natasha felt like Natalie was always the one with a parent, and more specifically, with her daddy.

The school year was coming to an end, and it looked like things would finally be back to normal. Natasha only had 4 weeks of her summer to dedicate to gymnastics, and Nathan had conditioning 3 times a week, but there were no games. They were both looking forward to their annual family vacation so they could all relax and be together without the hustle and bustle of all of their schedules. Karen and Will were excited too, but Natalie's schedule was about to put a huge dent in their plans.

Natalie ran into the house about three steps ahead of her dad. She was a ball of excitement. Will was anything but excited.

Natalie screamed, "Mom! Mom!"

"What is it, Natalie?" Karen asked anxiously.

Natalie was holding an opened gold envelope in her hands. When she reached Karen, she held it up in front of her and shouted, "THIS!"

Karen took the envelope from Natalie and pulled a slightly crumpled white sheet of paper out so she could see what all the excitement was about. Karen glanced at Will before reading it. He was now standing right behind Natalie.

Natalie squealed, "Hurry and read it, mom! Hurryyyyyyyyyy..."

Karen began reading silently. After a few seconds, her eyes left the paper and locked with Will's eyes. She had just seen what he'd known all along. This was why he wasn't as excited as Natalie. This is what the warning in his drooped shoulders was all about when he intentionally walked those few unenthused steps behind Natalie. After all of their years together, Karen and Will had become experts at reading each other's body language. Karen knew that Natalie had news worth sharing because of the sheer joy in her voice, but she knew her husband well, and she knew from all his gesturing that there would be some family requirements, and maybe even some family sacrifice and discomfort connected to Natalie's joy. She kept reading. When she finished, she leaned down and gave Natalie a big bear hug and rocked her from side to side. Natalie shrieked with delight and squeezed her mom right back.

Karen said, "I'm SO proud of you, honey! You did it!" Then she released Natalie from her embrace and said, "Let me hold on to the letter because your dad and I, of course, need to discuss this. You go on to your room, and we'll call you when dinner's ready, okay?"

"Okay, Mom!" Natalie cheered, and she ended it with a scream.

Will said to Natalie as she headed toward the stairs, "We're so proud of you, baby!"

Natalie said, "Thanks, Dad!" And she skipped up the stairs.

There was no way in the world they could allow themselves to take that excitement away from their baby girl. Wasn't this the reason they decided to enroll her at Brimmington? Didn't they want her to excel in music? Didn't they want her to learn and grow as a musician? Didn't they want her to experience things that she wouldn't have experienced if she wasn't at Brimmington? Being chosen as one of the only 3 middle school students in the state of Georgia to participate in the United States Youth Orchestra Convention in Washington D.C. was no small feat, and it wasn't an opportunity that any student passed up, even if the convention was during the week of their family vacation.

Karen and Will stopped for a moment to pray. They prayed about everything. They really needed the Lord's guidance on this one because everyone was looking forward to the family vacation. Nathan and Natasha had been so patient with all of the family's changes that school year. The newness of Natalie's schedule had brought a lot of strain on them, and Karen and Will wanted to celebrate their oldest two children for being as gracious as they had been with all the adjustments. They knew they couldn't cancel the vacation just because Natalie had been chosen to participate as 1st chair middle school violinist at the orchestra convention, but they couldn't keep Natalie from the convention either; it was too great an honor. They would have to figure out a way to make it all work, but they couldn't do it without God's guidance.

About an hour later, Nathan walked in through the kitchen door that opened up to the garage, and just a few minutes after him, Natasha entered through the front door. Nathan had been at basketball conditioning, and Natasha at a friend's house. They were both just in time for dinner. Natalie was excited! She couldn't wait to tell her brother and sister the big news, but Karen and Will warned her to let them be the ones to tell Nathan and Natasha. They knew they'd have to be very careful in explaining that Natalie's trip would not affect their family vacation. They even thought about not mentioning the dates for the convention and simply saying that it was in the summer, but they knew Nathan would ask. He was the one who was always concerned about dates and times.

After everyone had eaten, they sat around to talk for a few minutes like they always did. Natalie couldn't help but give her parents glances throughout all of the conversation; she wondered if they would ever say anything, and just as she was wondering for the millionth time if they'd say anything, Will began to speak. He'd been the least talkative that night, so when he finally said,

"Well, guys... Your mom and I have something we want to share with you," the table fell silent.

Will continued, "Natalie has been chosen as one of the only 3 students in the state of Georgia to participate in the United States Youth Orchestra Convention."

Natalie could hardly keep still in her seat. She danced from side to side in her chair. Nathan and Natasha wanted to congratulate Natalie and celebrate the way she was celebrating, but they knew from the grand way that their dad decided to make the announcement, that there was more to what he had just said. So they waited to hear the rest.

"The convention is this summer," Will said, and turned to look at Karen for some reassurance and for some extra support for what he was about to say that they both knew had to be said. Karen gave him a look of support with a nod, as if to say, *"We're in this together. Just spit it out."*

"We go on our family vacation to California June 11- 16. Natalie's convention is June 11-13 in D.C., so we are figuring out how to make it work," Will said.

He breathed a sigh of relief after he said those last words. He had finally gotten it out, and it was just as tough as he thought it would be. He hated disappointing his children.

At that point, seeing that Will had said all he had guts enough to say, Karen chimed in. She said, "Let us worry about that part. Two things are for sure: There is no way our vacation will be cancelled, and there is no way Natalie is missing this opportunity. We will figure it out. It may mean that one parent will have to go to D.C. and then Natalie and that parent will meet us in California after the conference. Your grandparents may even have to go to DC with Natalie while we're on vacation. We don't know. We're praying for the best thing for the family."

Karen and Will could see the hurt and disappointment in Nathan and Natasha's eyes. Natasha was staring down at her plate, and had been since her dad had finished talking. Nathan was looking straight ahead through the kitchen window. He refused to make eye contact with anyone at the table. And their disappointment wasn't because their parents would possibly have to split the trip. They definitely weren't pleased with that, but they were more upset about it being Natalie's schedule, again, that caused their parents to even have to do that. They really just wanted uninterrupted time with their parents.

After dinner, Natalie went up to her room, and like always, she practiced on her violin before bed. Her parents had her room semi sound proofed two years prior and it helped greatly, but she still wasn't allowed to play after 9:30 p.m. Everyone in the house knew, every night, when it was 9:30 because Natalie would play right up to the very last minute that she was allowed. That night was no different. At 9:30, the faint sound of Natalie's violin was no more. She was, without a doubt, fast asleep by 9:45. Her brother and sister, however, were wide-awake.

Natasha never stepped foot in Nathan's room because he strictly forbid it. Natasha was the same way about her room. This night, though, they didn't care. It's like that unspoken rule was never even in place. Natasha walked right into Nathan's room and sat on the foot of his bed. He didn't even flinch. He sat propped up on his pillows against the headboard of his bed, staring out of his bedroom window just like he'd been staring out of the kitchen window at dinner. For a few minutes, neither one of them said anything, but in the silence, they were both speaking. Their hurt filled the room, and it was loud and clear. Natasha began to cry; Nathan just let her have her moment. He didn't say anything because he honestly didn't know what to say. He didn't even know how to feel. He was trying to sort through his own emotions. Tears weren't falling from his eyes like his sister, but he thought sure there was some crying going on in his heart.

Natasha dried the last of her tears. She looked up and stared out of the same window that Nathan had been staring out of. She could feel his eyes move from the window to her back. He was waiting on her to speak. He knew it was coming.

Natasha took a deep breath and said, "I'm tired of it, Nate. I'm sick of everything having to change because she has to be all over the state and all over the country. I'm sick of mom not having time. I'm sick of dad acting like I don't exist, and if he does see me, he's too tired to talk to me because her schedule and her events and her *everything* has worn him out. It's like our parents aren't our parents. They're *her* parents."

Natasha began to talk faster. It was obvious that she had gone from disappointed to angry in a matter of seconds.

"Has she missed even one show? NO! She hasn't missed anything this year." Natasha got up from the bed and started to pace back and forth so she could now look at Nathan while she talked.

"I remember the time you had to miss a game because of Granddad's birthday party. That game was one of the big games too. But they said family was more important. They said there would be other games and it wouldn't hurt if you missed one. And sure, your team hated that you weren't there and your coach threw a fit, but at that next game, it was like that never happened. And do you remember that time I had to miss two days of practice when we were preparing for that meet against the North Carolina YTG League? I missed because dad was being inducted into that hall of fame for his company in Nashville and all of the family had to be there. Family came first when it came to us, but it doesn't come first with Natalie. Why can't she miss her convention because of our family trip if family comes first? Uuuuuuuuuugh!!"

Natalie grunted and balled up both her fists and pressed them into the sides of her legs. All the while, Nathan just watched her pace and listened to her vent. Even if he wanted to say anything, he couldn't. Natasha wouldn't let him get a word in. She was angry, and she needed to let it all out.

"I just wanna take her violin and break it into a million pieces! Uuuuuuuuugh! I'm sick of it!"

Nathan had to say something then. He didn't like hearing her say that she wanted to destroy Natalie's instrument, even if she was only saying it because she was angry.

"Alright, Tasha," Nathan said. "Chill. Don't say stuff you don't mean."

"Oh no, I definitely mean it, Nate." She stopped pacing and looked Nathan in his eyes. "I just wanna break it into a million pieces. If she doesn't have the violin to play with, she won't be able to go on the trip. Problem solved."

Nathan said, "Are you even serious right now? Do you really think destroying her violin would solve the problem?" Nathan chuckled. "I can't even believe you don't see how dumb that is."

Natasha walked to the door and looked over at Nathan as she grabbed the doorknob. She said, "It'll work."

She walked out, and closed the door behind her. She walked to Natalie's bedroom door. She stood outside of the door for a few minutes, replaying the conversation with Nathan over and over in her head. She kept thinking back to dinner and how her dad didn't even ask how she felt about it all. He didn't ask if she was okay, and even in looking at her face that clearly said she wasn't okay, he did nothing. She began to cry again, and the pain she felt made her angry again. She turned the knob on Natalie's door and slowly opened the door. Natalie always slept with the violin leaned up against the footboard of her bed. Natasha walked right over to the violin case and grabbed it. She laid it on the floor, gently opened the case, and removed the violin and its bow. She glanced up at Natalie. Natalie was sound asleep. Natasha closed the case just as gently as she had opened it and leaned the case back up against the footboard. She grabbed the violin and bow and took it to her room.

At that moment she really was angry enough to completely destroy Natalie's violin, but she didn't. She sat the violin on her bed, took two steps back and just looked at it. She wished she could close her eyes and make it disappear. In her eyes, that violin was the cause of her pain. Natalie's school and the schedule it forced her to keep with the violin that she loved so much—all of that was the problem, she thought. Natasha couldn't even see that the problem—her problem—was much deeper than that. She wasn't sure what she was going to do with the violin. She hadn't really thought that out, but the more she stood there and looked at it, the more ideas she had. If she didn't know anything else, she knew she had to hide it. After about 15 minutes, she finally decided to put the violin in her big oversized gym bag that she took with her to out-of-town meets. It fit perfectly with room to spare.

The next morning, Nathan and Natasha were gearing up to head to Saturday Basketball League at their church. Natasha wasn't as good a basketball player as Nathan, but she loved to play with her brother on the church team. It was one of the things they liked to do together. Nathan was dressed and ready to go, but like every Saturday, he was waiting on Natasha who he said took 2 extra hours to get ready just to go and sweat. He just didn't understand why she had to do so much to go and play basketball. Nathan yelled up to Natasha's room from the bottom of the stairs, "Come ON, Tasha! Why do you have to get pretty to play ball? Can we leave some time today?"

Natasha yelled back, "I'm coming! My God! You act like we're late or something!"

"We will be if you don't hurry up!"

Natasha was busy trying to determine if she should leave Natalie's violin in her gym bag or if she should return it to Natalie's room like it had never left. Natasha was still angry. She was still hurt. She still wanted Natalie to suffer, but deep down in her heart, even though she hated Natalie's schedule and hated how much attention Natalie had been getting from their dad, she still loved her sister, and she didn't want to completely destroy her instrument. BUT...if the violin disappeared for a little while and Natalie couldn't find it, that could be just as destructive and painful as actually having it broken into pieces. If the violin went missing, it could cause Natalie to feel some of the hurt that Natasha and Nathan were feeling. Natasha knew that Natalie would freak out if she couldn't find her violin, so that was her plan: take the violin out of the house so Natalie can't find it. Shake her up a little bit.

Natalie stayed home on Saturdays because there were no Saturday activities at church that interested her. She would either run errands with her mom or help her dad around the house. There was no doubt that Natalie would venture to her room at some point to play her violin because she ALWAYS did with any free moment she had. She would go to practice in her room after she and her mom got in from running errands, but the violin would be gone! This gave Natasha a weird sense of relief.

Natasha grabbed a change of clothes and all of her other essentials and tossed them in the bag on top of the violin. She tossed the bag around her neck and across her body and hustled down the stairs where the rest of the family was waiting.

Nathan said, "It's about time!"

Natasha punched his arm and said, "Shut it, Nate!"

FAMILY TIES, PART 1

Family Ties: Day 1 Study

ANGER

*The story continues on Day 2.
Complete today's study and pick up the story tomorrow.

There is no doubt that Natasha was hurt. She was hurt because she wasn't getting as much attention from her parents as she once had. She was hurt because she didn't feel important. She was hurt because her family didn't feel like her family anymore. She was so hurt that she became angry, and although anger can be a healthy emotion because it usually shows that we care about something, if it's not handled properly, it can be pretty dangerous. Natasha, without a doubt, is in dangerous territory at this point in the story because she's not handling her anger properly.

Read Ephesians 4:26. Write it below.

_____

_____

God's word tells us that we should not sin in our anger. It does not say that we won't get angry, because we definitely will. It just says that we shouldn't sin in our anger. Remember, anger can be a healthy emotion. For instance, MADD (Mothers Against Drunk Driving) is an organization that was formed by an angry mother and some other angry supporter mothers. Their children were struck by drunk drivers or were involved in car accidents caused by drunk drivers where they were either severely injured or killed. These mothers' anger didn't cause them to sin, though. They didn't lash out and hurt the people who hurt or took their children from them. Their anger actually caused them to do the exact opposite. They formed MADD to raise awareness about the dangers of drunk driving. They used their anger to support other mothers and families that lost loved ones to drunk driving. They raised money, they held rallies, and did whatever else they could to make sure stricter laws were passed to punish those who were found driving under the influence of drugs or alcohol. Their anger brought about positive change in the United States. What happens when we don't use our anger for positivity, though? Unfortunately, when our anger doesn't motivate us to do something positive, and when we don't have a strategy to deal with our anger, we sin. We will, 100% of the time, say, think and/or do something that does not please God if we don't have strategies to deal with our anger. Natasha is an example.

Natasha started off well when she first expressed her hurt. Who did she express her hurt feelings to? What did she do? What did she say?

_____

_____

_____

Family Ties, Part 1

What did Natasha do wrong? How could she have handled things differently?

Natasha did well by venting to Nathan. Talking through hurt is probably the best strategy for cooling down and moving farther and farther away from sin. But Natasha went from being hurt to being angry. Nathan thought that she was all talk because she was upset, so he didn't do much to help cool her down, but Natasha could have done some things herself to keep herself away from hurting someone else.

Here are some practical things that you can do if you ever find yourself so angry that you want to hurt someone or do something that you know is not pleasing to God.

Stories THAT TEACH Girls

1. Talk to someone. Talk about how you feel, and don't stop talking about it until you no longer feel like hurting them. Talk about it until you no longer feel like saying or doing something that doesn't please God.

2. Go into a place where you can be alone. This can be your bedroom, a bathroom, outside in the backyard or on the porch. When you go there, PRAY. Talk to the Lord. He already knows what happened to hurt you because He was there. Tell Him how you feel, and ask Him to comfort you and show you how to deal with it. Remain alone until you no longer feel like hurting them. Remain alone until you no longer feel like saying or doing something that you know is not pleasing to God.

3. When you go to your "alone space", tell people around you that you just need some time alone to cool off. Don't just storm off, and don't yell. People usually understand that being alone is a cooling off strategy.

4. Take a walk if you're able. There's nothing like burning off anger energy with a walk.

5. Take a shower. A shower has the same effect as a walk. It helps burn off anger energy.

6. Journal. If you don't already have a journal, consider getting one to write out your feelings. Something magical happens when you write all of your feelings out on paper. It's cleansing. And it's much better than

putting it on social media! That is the LAST place you want to run when you're angry. You WILL regret it! Mark my words!

There is no doubt in my mind that Natasha would have had a change of heart if she would have spent some time alone. Time alone would have allowed her to look beyond that moment. She would have had time to think through her "taking the violin" scheme and all of the things that could have happened. When we're angry and we're thinking of things to do to get back at someone, it's natural to play out all possible outcomes. With time, she would've seen that Natalie wouldn't have been the only one hurt. She would've seen that there was no way that anyone outside of the house could've taken the violin. If a full investigation would have taken place, it was going to come down to the people who lived in the house. But she didn't think that far. Her brain was clouded with anger so she just acted. She went right to Natalie's door in the heat of her anger and that was the danger. That's when she fell into sin. She intentionally did something to hurt someone else, and God is not pleased with that.

Read James 1:19-20.
God's word says that we should be
- **quick to _____.**

- **slow to _____.**

- **slow to become _____.**

And this is because man's (people's) anger does not bring about the righteousness that God desires from us. This verse is a warning. Be careful when you're angry. Find a way to deal with it so you do not sin.

Family Ties, Part 2
by Iantha Ussin (Ms. I.)

Stories THAT TEACH Girls

Everyone piled into the family van. Nathan and Natasha were dropped off at the church, and Natalie ran errands with Karen and Will before the three of them headed back home to work in the yard and the garage. After about an hour in the garage, Natalie had done everything her dad asked her to do, so she went up to her room to practice her violin. She went to the foot of her bed where the violin case was leaning up against the footboard. She grabbed the case and placed it on the bed. When she opened it, it was empty. For a second, it seemed strange, but Natalie would sometimes leave the violin out if she played up until the very last minute before she would go to bed at night. She remembered that she had done that the night before, so maybe the violin was on her desk or on her desk chair. She'd done that several times before. Natalie walked over to her desk. No violin. She pulled out the desk chair. No violin. And her concern began to rise. Those 3 places were literally the only places she would ever have her violin.

Natalie walked back over to the foot of her bed and looked at the floor. Her violin wasn't on the floor where the case had been. She knelt down and looked under the bed. The violin wasn't there. She had only one plastic bin under her bed with winter sweaters in it. She moved the bin over to see if the violin was behind it. It wasn't. Under her bed was spotless. There was nothing there. Natalie stood and looked over at the desk again, and tears began to form in her eyes. Where could it be?

She dashed over to her closet and pulled the door open. She got down on her knees again and lifted every bag, every shoe, and anything else that was on her closet floor to see if the violin was there. She knew it was ridiculous to even be down there because she could see her closet floor without having to lift a thing. There was hardly anything on her floor, but in that moment, because her mind was so fixed on finding her violin, no way of searching seemed wrong. She was determined to find it!

After searching the floor, she searched the shelves. Nothing. She slammed the closet door shut and looked at her bed. At that point, Natalie's face was wet with tears. She saw the opened empty case on her bed and thought, *"Maybe it's under the covers. Maybe I fell asleep with it."* Natalie tossed the case to the floor and yanked her comforter up in the air, forming a bubble cloud so she could look under it. As the comforter cloud was up in the air, Natalie scanned from the top of her bed near her pillows, to the foot of the bed. There was nothing there. She let the cloud fall on her as she dove onto her sheets. She patted the sheets down over and over again, hoping to feel the instrument somewhere in the bed, but it wasn't there. She curled up in her bed, completely covered by the comforter and cried. She felt helpless. She was hurt, and she was definitely confused. What had happened? She knew she had just played her violin the night before. She went to sleep. She woke up, showered, had breakfast, and took off with the family. When she returned home with her parents, she worked in the garage, and then she went back up to her room to THIS! When did it happen? *How* could it have happened? There was no explanation.

Natalie gathered herself. Her body was weak from crying. She made her way downstairs to her mom who was in the laundry room. As soon as her mom saw her face she said, "Natalie! What's wrong? Why are you crying?"

Through tears, Natalie said, "I can't find my violin." She starting crying hysterically again.

"What do you mean you can't find your violin?" her mom asked. This seemed completely berserk to her mom. Natalie was only 9, but she was very responsible. She hadn't lost anything a day in her life, and because of her love for her instruments, her mom knew there was no way she had lost her violin.

"Honey. Stop crying so I can hear you," Karen pleaded. What do you mean you can't find it? Is it not in your room? Have you looked all over your room? You were playing it right before bed last night. Where else could it be?"

"I know, Mom, but it's not in my room. I looked everywhere in my room," Natalie blubbered.

Karen said, "Okay. Come on. Let's go look together."

They walked upstairs to Natalie's room, and when they got to the door, Karen could see that Natalie had looked everywhere. The room was not its usual tidy self. Natalie sat on the bed and watched her mom search every place she had already searched. When her mom finished searching, she turned to Natalie and said, "So how is the case here, but no violin?"

Natalie said, "I don't know, Mom. I opened the case when I came up from working with daddy and it wasn't in there."

"I'm not understanding how it could be here last night and not be here this morning, Natalie. We have to come up with something better than that."

"But Mom, I'm not lying." Natalie began to cry again.

Karen knew when Natalie was being honest, and she could see that she was too hurt to be making anything up. These tears were like no tears she'd ever seen before. Natalie was crying heart-wrenching tears.

Karen called Will up to Natalie's room. She explained everything that had happened up to that point. She told him everything Natalie had told her. He, too, was in disbelief. Will suggested that they search Nathan and Natasha's rooms and every other room upstairs in the house. They did. They didn't find the violin. They then searched the rest of the house, and to their dismay, there was no violin anywhere in the house. They were all heartbroken. And tired. And confused. How in the world had this happened?

Natalie was exhausted from crying. She pretty much cried herself to sleep. While she napped, Karen and Will talked about the missing violin. They thought of all the possibilities, and the only logical question in their minds was: Did someone come into the house and take it?

They thought back to their morning. They were rushing to get out of the house that morning. Did they do like they have done a few times before and forget to set the alarm? They couldn't remember if they had or not, and even if they hadn't, why in the world would someone come into their home and leave every other valuable thing and take only the violin and bow and leave the case? It just didn't make sense.

A couple hours later, Nathan and Natasha walked into the living room where their parents sat. It was evident that they were disturbed by something. It was written all over their faces. Nathan, who was always concerned about his family, asked, "What's up, Mom? You guys look worn out."

Karen answered him without even looking up. She said, "We are."

Will chimed in and said, "You two wouldn't know anything about Nat's violin would you? It is nowhere in this house. We've looked everywhere."

Nathan said, "What? Are you sure? Did she look under her bed? It's always at the foot of her bed."

Will said, "We looked everywhere, son. When I say it's not in the house, it's not here."

"Well, Dad, I don't know where it can be. That's crazy!"

Nathan walked over to the couch to sit next to his mom who had obviously been crying. He hugged her, and she began to cry again. Nathan asked, "Where's Natalie?"

Will answered, "She's been crying all day, so she's exhausted. She's been asleep for a couple hours."

Natasha said nothing. She just let the conversation go on between her brother and her parents. They kept talking. No one asked Natasha anything else because they were all too engaged in trying to figure out how it could have happened. She walked upstairs to her room, put her gym bag down, and sat in her desk chair. She swiveled around in her chair and looked at the bag in the middle of her floor. She wanted to say something, but saying she had taken the violin would also mean admitting to being the cause of her parents' anguish. She didn't want that. She didn't think that trying to hurt Natalie would hurt her parents too. She just wanted Natalie to feel the pain, but now she had the entire family in a mess.

Nathan had completely forgotten about the night before because usually, after he vents to Natasha, it's over. And after Natasha vents to him, it's over. He had forgotten how upset Natasha was about everything. He had forgotten that she cried because she was so frustrated with Natalie's school schedule and how it altered their family's schedule. He had forgotten that Natasha said she wanted to break Natalie's violin into a million pieces. None of that came back to his remembrance until he walked upstairs to go to his room and passed Natasha's room on the way. She was sitting in her desk chair staring at her gym bag, seemingly in a totally different world. Nathan called her name, and she didn't answer. She just kept staring. He called her again, and she jumped. She turned around and looked at him and a single tear ran down her cheek. Right then, he could see in her eyes that she'd done something. He could see that she knew something, and at that moment, he remembered what she had said the night before.

Nathan walked to Natasha and stood next to her. He whispered, "You didn't!"

He never thought she would. That's why he didn't pay it any real attention. He thought it was all talk. They'd both talked about doing stupid things before, but they never carried any of it out.

Natasha said, "I didn't think it would go this far."

Nathan said, "What DID you think, Tash? I mean, that was stupid. Did you break the violin? Where is it?"

"No, I didn't break it! It's right there."

Natasha pointed to her gym bag. They were both whispering.

"Well, you need to put it back," Nathan demanded.

"But if I put it back, they'll know I did it."

"Well, how long do you plan to let this go?" Nathan asked.

"I don't know," Natasha said through her tears. "I was just trying to make Natalie feel like we've been feeling. I wasn't trying to hurt anybody else."

"This is probably your worst, Tash. I don't know what to tell you, but mom and dad just said that they have 3 days to let the convention committee know if Natalie will be going to D.C. or not. If she's not, her spot goes to some other kid. You better figure out what you're gonna do."

Nathan starting walking toward Natasha's bedroom door. He turned and looked at her before he left the room.

He said, "You got your wish. You hurt her. But you need to know that you may be killing her dream too."

Nathan walked out to his room and closed the door behind him.

Karen and Will were still in the living room in disbelief. They decided to pray. They didn't want their baby girl to miss out on an opportunity of a lifetime; she had worked too hard. They knew if Natalie was going to attend the convention, she would need a violin, and they didn't make any financial plans to purchase any instruments, especially not an expensive violin. They had money set aside for vacation so they could really enjoy themselves, and they didn't want to use their vacation money for a violin. Even trying to make the D.C. trip happen was a strain, so buying a violin on top of that was just too much. Karen and Will asked the Lord for guidance. They asked Him for wisdom. They didn't know what to do, but they believed the Lord would come through like He always had.

The next two days, Natalie was in a state of mild depression. She moped. She was quiet. She wasn't herself. Her violin was gone, and so was her excitement. She didn't want to go to D.C. anymore. She didn't even want to go on the family vacation. Karen and Will couldn't stand to see her that way. Natalie's violin was just as much a part of her as her eyes and ears were. Karen and Will knew there was only one brand violin that Natalie would use. She had tried others, but they just weren't right, and the brand she liked happened to be the most expensive. But after prayer and much discussion, they decided that they would sacrifice some of their family savings to get Natalie another violin. They wanted her to make the trip and live out one of her dreams.

Natasha overheard her parents on two different occasions talking about how they were going to cut back on some things so they could get Natalie another violin. They talked about how they hadn't dug into their savings account in over 4 years and how it may hurt some of their other plans, but it was worth it, especially since the missing violin was a complete mystery to everyone in the house. They had one more day before they had to let the convention committee know if Natalie would be attending, so they had to make some decisions and make them quickly.

Natasha couldn't take it anymore. She had already caused enough trouble and caused her entire family enough pain. It broke her heart to hear her parents talk about doing something that they wouldn't have had to do if it wasn't for her. She felt awful! She gathered up her courage through her tears, grabbed the violin from her gym bag, and walked downstairs to the kitchen where her parents were. Karen was on the phone with Ms. Weldon. She was getting information from her about the type of violin she would need to get for Natalie and the specifics she needed to look for with the strings and the bow. Right as Karen was ending the call with Ms. Weldon, she turned around and saw Natasha standing in the kitchen doorway with Natalie's violin.

Karen just stood there with the phone in her hand and looked at Natasha for a few seconds. She was happy to see the violin, but she was confused. Was it Natalie's? Why did Natasha have it? Where had it been? And why was Natasha crying?

Will was at the stove preparing dinner. He turned around to get something from the pantry and saw Natasha standing there with the violin in her hand.

He said, "Well, Hallelujah! Where was it?"

He didn't look at Natasha's face and see what Karen saw. Karen knew that something was wrong. She knew her children, and she knew Natasha had something to do with the mystery surrounding Natalie's missing violin. She knew those tears were tears of sorrow, but she didn't want to deal with the sorrow just yet. She wanted to deal with the when, where, why and how of the matter. Karen didn't even say anything to Natasha. She just walked to the table, pulled out a chair, and motioned for Natasha to sit in it. Natasha walked over to the table and sat in the chair. Karen took the violin and bow from Natasha's hand and handed it to Will. Will examined the violin and bow, and sure enough, it was Natalie's. Her initials were inscribed on both the bow and the violin.

Karen sat in the chair across from Natasha. Will placed the violin and bow on the counter and sat in the chair next to Karen so they could both be facing Natasha.

Karen asked, "So what happened?"

Natasha hesitated. She knew she had to say something, but knowing she had to say it didn't make it any easier to speak. In fact, knowing she had to reveal how foolishly she had behaved made it harder to speak.

"I didn't want anything to go this far. I didn't even think it would. I took Natalie's violin so she could miss it for a little while because I knew it would hurt her. And I wanted her to feel like we were feeling."

Will asked, "Who is *we*?"

"Nate and I," she replied.

"So Nate knew you took the violin?" Will asked.

"No, sir. He didn't. I told him night before last and he told me I needed to tell you."

Karen looked at Will. Then, they looked back at Natasha so she could finish talking.

Natasha said, "I put the violin in my gym bag and took it to church with me on Saturday. I knew she would look for it and I knew it would hurt her when it wasn't there."

Karen asked, "But what do you mean you wanted her to feel like you and Nate had been feeling?"

"Well," she paused, "Natalie's schedule became everybody's schedule."

Natasha looked down at her feet.

"You forgot about us. You never missed Nate's games before, but when Natalie started at BSA, you did."

Natasha started to cry a little harder. She said, "And daddy never missed any of my meets, but now he does because he's always with Natalie."

Natasha wiped some tears from her face.

"You guys never miss anything for Natalie."

"So you thought you would take the most important thing to her so she could feel the pain you felt?" Karen asked.

Natasha just looked down at her feet. She didn't even answer.

Will said, "Tash, why didn't you just talk to us? We talk about everything."

"Not anymore, Dad. We don't talk like that anymore because we don't see each other enough to talk about anything."

Karen chimed in and said, "Oh, I completely understand that you're hurt because we've had to divide your 2 parents among 3 children, but it certainly does not excuse the pain and frustration you've caused this family, Natasha. I applaud you for stepping up and admitting your wrong, but you know there will be consequences. I can't even believe you would do something like this."

Will said, "Yes, honey. This isn't the way we handle things. Natalie's schedule is not Natalie's fault. Hurting her was not the way to handle your hurt. Your hurt needed to be discussed with us. And it sounds like your frustration and maybe even a little anger is with me."

Will got up and walked to Natasha's chair. He knelt down in front of her and hugged her. She sobbed in his arms.

It was true. She was hurting because she wasn't getting the attention from her dad that she was used to. She missed the time they would spend together before things got busy with Natalie. She missed the talks they would have on the ride home after her meets. She missed seeing him on the bench next to her coach, cheering her on, if she was having a good day on the floor, or a bad day. She didn't feel close to him anymore, and it hurt. She didn't feel loved by him anymore, and she wanted to. She was once the apple of his eye, but it was feeling like Natalie had taken that place.

Will held Natasha until she stopped crying. He knew he would have to have a really good talk with her, and later that evening, he did. Although what Natasha did was wrong and received punishment, it was a wake up call for Karen and Will. They were able to evaluate how much time they were spending with Natalie, and they were able to see just how much it had taken away from their time with Nathan and Natasha. They had to admit that they'd fallen off because Nathan and Natasha were older and a bit more independent. Natasha's stunt helped them to see that all of their children need them, no matter how old. It was a strange time for the family, but it was a good time. They needed to change some things around so each child could have just as much attention and support as the next.

After Karen and Will talked everything over with the kids and asked for their forgiveness, things felt like new. The tension that had been in the house for months was lifted. Natasha asked for Natalie's forgiveness and Natalie was too excited not to give it to her. She was grateful to have her violin back and to be going to D.C. And so was everyone else. They decided, as a family, to support Natalie at the convention and spend their vacation week exploring the nation's capital.

Family Ties: Day 2

ENVY

Natasha's hurt turned to anger, but her hurt, from the very beginning, was fueled by envy. That's where it all began.

Dictionary.com defines *envy* as *a feeling of discontent with regard to another's advantages, success, possessions, etc.* In other words, if you're envious, you want what someone else has.

Natasha was used to being her daddy's only girl. She was the apple of his eye. From the time Natasha was 4 years old, he never missed any of her gymnastics meets and he was her biggest encourager. Natasha got less time with her dad when Natalie started attending BSA and having all of her performances because he would spend most of his time with Natalie. Natasha became envious. She didn't want Natalie to take her daddy away from her, but that's exactly what she felt like Natalie was doing. Natasha's envy caused her to be hurt. Then she became angry, and we already know what happened when she got angry.

Let's look at what **James 3:13-16 (NIV)** says: *"Who is wise and understanding among you? Let him show it by his good life, by deeds done in the humility that comes from wisdom. But if you harbor bitter <u>envy</u> and <u>selfish</u> ambition in your hearts, do not boast about it or deny the truth. Such 'wisdom' does not come from heaven but is earthly, unspiritual, of the devil. For where you have envy and selfish ambition, there you find <u>disorder and every evil practice</u>".* (underlining is for emphasis)

Family Ties. Part 2

What was Natasha envious of? Use evidence from the story to tell how you know.

_____

_____

_____

_____

How was Natasha selfish? Use evidence from the story to tell how you know.

_____

_____

_____

_____

  The passage in James 3 clearly tells us not to harbor (let stay in our hearts) envy or selfish ambition. Natasha was envious of her dad's relationship with Natalie and the time they spent together, and because she selfishly wanted her dad all to herself, she caused disorder in their home. James 3 says that envy and selfishness will bring disorder. It also says that every evil practice is present wherever there's envy and selfishness, and Natasha taking her sister's violin to hurt her was certainly evil practice.

There's an example of envious siblings in the Bible. Jacob and Esau were twins; Esau was the oldest, and Jacob the youngest. In those days, the birthright went to the oldest son when the father died. This meant the oldest son would inherit whatever the father had gained over his lifetime—houses, cattle, business, etc. The Bible tells us that Jacob and Esau's father, Issac, loved Esau, and their mother, Rebekah, loved Jacob. Issac was pleased to give the birthright to Esau because he favored him, and Jacob was envious of that. Jacob wanted the birthright.

One day, when Esau got home from his workday in the fields, he was extremely hungry. He saw that Jacob had prepared a meal. Esau asked Jacob for some food, and Jacob, seeing how hungry (and a bit desperate) Esau was, told him that he would give him food if he would sell him his birthright. Esau swore in an oath to give Jacob the birthright. It wasn't until later, though, that Jacob and his mother, Rebekah, plotted to get the birthright from Esau.

Read Genesis 27.

Now, it was clear that Jacob wasn't the only one who wanted the birthright. Remember, the bible said that Issac loved Esau, but Rebekah loved Jacob. Rebekah, like any mother, wanted what was best for her children, but she especially wanted it for the child she loved the most. When Rebekah saw an opportunity for Jacob to get the birthright, she immediately put a plan into action to get it.

Rebekah overheard Issac telling Esau that he would give him the birthright over a meal later that day. Issac was old in age and nearing death, so he wanted to pass on the inheritance before he died. He was losing his sight because of his old age, and that was what Rebekah used to trick him. When Esau would bring him the meal later that day, Issac would have to touch him to know that he was Esau because he wouldn't be able to see him. Rebekah told Jacob to make his arms hairy like Esau's by using an animal's fur. This, she knew, would make him appear to be Esau. Jacob explained that he would bring a curse upon himself if he did that, but Rebekah said, "My son, let the curse fall on me." Jacob felt a little uncomfortable, but he was envious enough to continue with the plan. He had gotten a promise in an oath from Esau, and he was ready to claim what was his.

The plan worked. When Issac called for Esau, Jacob presented himself. He lied to his father and said that he was Esau. He even lied about the food he'd prepared. He was just engaging in all kind of evil practice! Issac noticed that Jacob's voice was not Esau's, but he had managed to trick him with the hairy arms. Issac thought that Jacob's arm was Esau's, so he went on to bestow the birthright upon Jacob, promising in an oath to give him everything that he had worked for in his lifetime, and promising that Jacob would rule over many generations.

Although Rebekah did most of the planning, Jacob went through with it. He could have decided not to, but envy and the selfishness to have all of his father's blessings and wealth to himself wouldn't let him. He wanted that birthright! And he engaged in evil practice after evil practice to get it. After everything was said and done, it caused disorder in their family, just as the passage in James said envy and selfishness would.

Stories THAT TEACH Girls

When Esau learned that Jacob had taken his birthright, the tables turned. Now Esau was envious even though he agreed to give Jacob the birthright. His envy, like Natasha's, turned to anger and he tried to kill Jacob. Yes! He tried to kill him! Jacob had to flee and live in another city to avoid being killed. He and his mother's evil plotting was the cause of the breakup of their family.

If you read on through the book of Genesis, you'll see that Jacob's trickery caught up with him. He ended up reaping (getting) what he sowed (gave) when he was tricked into marrying a woman he did not love. *(You'll learn about sowing and reaping later this week.)*

Envy, like anger, is a real emotion. Sometimes, good can come from anger. Like you learned earlier this week, there is a such thing as righteous anger. Nothing good can come from envy, though. If the feeling of envy is not shut down immediately, it will 100% of the time end up in some evil practice and cause all kinds of disorder. God's word says so. If you find yourself envious of someone or what someone else has, take that feeling to the Lord in prayer.

Family Ties, Part 2

Family Ties: Day 3

DISHONESTY

We learned in a previous study that the Lord hates a lying tongue, and yesterday's story about Jacob and Esau is a good example of why He does.

Let's revisit Genesis 27, but this time we'll be looking specifically at Jacob's and Rebekah's dishonesty.

Explain how Jacob and Rebekah were dishonest.

_____

_____

_____

_____

_____

Jacob and Rebekah **decided in their hearts** to lie to Issac to get Esau's birthright, and after they plotted and planned out their lie, they actually went through with it. They made sure to prepare a meal that would please Issac. They took extra measures to change Jacob's identity so he could appear to be

Esau. Jacob even lied directly to Issac's face! When Issac asked, *"Are you really my son Esau?"* Jacob replied, *"I am,"* knowing that he really wasn't! They went on and on with the lie until they got what they wanted. BUT the pleasure of getting what they wanted only lasted for a time. It wasn't long before their lie backfired and caused a lot of pain.

Read Genesis 27:30-34.

Verse 33 says Issac trembled violently when he learned that Jacob had lied to him. Verse 34 says that Esau burst out with a loud and bitter cry. The dishonesty caused them great pain. You already know from what we read yesterday that Esau was so angry that he wanted to kill Jacob. Jacob had to flee to another town to avoid being killed. All because of a lie!

Natasha's dishonesty caused the same kind of pain. Natasha **decided in her heart** to cause Natalie pain. Like Jacob and Rebekah, Natasha plotted and planned and took extra measures to make sure Natalie's violin was out of sight. And then the lying and dishonesty began.

When Nathan and Natasha got home from playing basketball at their church, their parents were obviously hurt about Natalie's violin being gone. Explain how Natasha was dishonest in that moment.

_____

_____

Family Ties, Part 2

_____

_____

_____

Natasha didn't flat out lie, but she didn't tell the truth either. She was SILENT, and that WAS the lie. She never spoke up. She never said that she had the violin. She watched her family suffer. She saw their pain, and she did nothing about it. She continued on hiding the truth, and for a few days it turned her family upside down.

Explain Natalie's reaction to her violin being gone.

_____

_____

_____

Poor Natalie was a wreck, and it was all because of her sister's dishonesty. Natasha went on for days, lying about not knowing anything about the violin while Natalie walked around the house depressed. Natasha's dishonesty upset Nathan too. He couldn't believe that she had actually gone through with targeting Natalie's violin. He was disappointed in her behavior and how she knew it affected Natalie but still said nothing to their parents. And Karen and Will were a wreck because of her dishonesty too. They were trying their best to figure out a way to make vacation work, make Natalies's trip to D.C. work AND, after Natasha's dishonesty, they were trying to figure out how to purchase a very expensive violin.

Jacob and Rebekah's lies affected their entire family. Natasha's dishonesty affected her whole family. This is why the Lord hates a lying tongue. Lies cause pain and destroy, and when they go on and on, that's where the real breakdown occurs.

Family Ties, Part 2

Family Ties: Day 4
PROVERBS STUDY

The book of Proverbs talks a lot about fools. A *fool*, by definition, is *a weak-minded person who lacks judgment or sense.* Today, we will look at what the Word of God says specifically about a fool and his/her anger.

Read Proverbs 29:11. Write it below.

_____

_____

Read Proverbs 12:16. Write it below.

_____

_____

Both of these verses show us what a fool does when they're angry, and what a wise person does when they're angry, so today's message is simple.

DON'T BE A FOOL!

Stories THAT TEACH Girls

Don't be someone who is weak-minded. Don't be someone who doesn't have any Godly sense. God's word has given us the sense we need to represent Him and represent Him well, so take heed. When you're angry, don't lash out. Don't blurt out all your thoughts. Don't make a scene. Don't get out of character. Exercise wisdom, and stay in control.

FAMILY TIES, PART 2

Family Ties: Day 5
THE CHALLENGE/ACTIVITY

Sometimes the family members that live under the same roof with you are the hardest to get along with. You get in each other's space. You get in each other's way. You get on each other's nerves. There's no doubt that in a moment of anger, you've said or done something to someone in your home that you're not proud of. There's no doubt that in a moment of anger, you've done something or said something hurtful. We all have.

Today, you need to write a letter to someone in your family that you've said or done something hurtful to when you were angry. If you've already sincerely apologized to them, still write a letter as another gesture to let them know that you really are sorry for what you said or did. If you never apologized, now is the time.

Right now, as you're reading this, you're thinking about that incident. You're thinking about that time. And even if it didn't seem like a big deal to them, you know that it wasn't right because the Lord is dealing with your heart right now. Write them the letter. In the letter, be sure to mention the incident. Tell them exactly what you're apologizing for. Include reference to scriptures we've studied this week that have helped you to realize that you were wrong. Ask for their forgiveness and ask them to help you honor God the next time you're angry.

Stories THAT TEACH Girls

Family Ties: Day 6

THE SEEDS YOU SOW

Read Galatians 6:7-8. Write it below.

_____

_____

_____

_____

God's word is clear when it says that a man (people) will reap what he sows. Another way of saying this is a man (people) will get back what he gives. It's a basic law of nature. Think about a farmer since a farmer is who the writer is referencing in this passage. When a farmer plants (sows) apple seeds, he expects to get (reap) an apple tree with apples, and he gets it. If a farmer sows watermelon seeds, he expects to reap watermelons from the ground, and he gets them. It has always been, and will always be that way. It's how God designed it.

The same is true for our thoughts and behavior. The Lord makes that clear in His word too. This passage in Galatians says that if we sow to please the sinful nature, or if we give ourselves to sin, we will reap destruction. Likewise, if we sow to please the Spirit (God), or if we give ourselves to the things that please God, we will reap eternal life. And wasn't this true for Natasha? When she found herself hurt and angry, she ended up in sin. She intentionally did something to hurt her sister, and when she did, she definitely hurt her sister, but she hurt her parents too, and that ended up hurting her in the end. If we could sum up what happened to Natasha in one phrase, we could say, **The hurt Natasha gave, was the hurt Natasha eventually received.** This could be the same for you and me. If we give hurt, we'll get hurt. If we give love, we'll get love. If we give friendship, we'll get friendship. If we give money, we'll get money.

Read Luke 6:37-38. This passage says:

- **Do not judge, and** _____.

- **Do not condemn, and** _____.

- **Forgive, and** _____.

- **Give, and** _____.

- **For with the measure you use,** _____.

Whatever you sow—be it love, hate, forgiveness, unforgiveness—it will be given back unto you, in the same measure that you sowed it.

Read Proverbs 26:27. Write it on the next page.

Stories THAT TEACH Girls

_____

_____

    This was definitely the case for Natasha. She "dug a pit" for her sister to fall into, but she ended up falling into that pit herself. The stone she tried to roll onto Natalie ended up rolling right onto her.

    Don't let this be your story. The Lord has made it clear that what we sow, we **WILL** reap. There's no question about it. Be careful that you sow love. Sow friendship. Sow kindness and gentleness. Sow respect. Sow all of the things that please the Lord and see won't you reap them!

Family Ties: Day 7
JOURNAL

From this story, we learned about anger, envy, selfishness, dishonesty, and sowing good seeds, but there were some other topics and themes inside the story. One of them was love, and particularly the love inside of family. What did you learn about love and family from this story?

_____

_____

_____

_____

_____

_____

Stories That Teach Girls

DAY 29

WHAT IS QUIET TIME?

What happens now that you've finished the very last study of the last story in this book? What do you do now that there are no more stories to read and learn from?

YOU KEEP SPENDING TIME IN GOD'S WORD EVERY DAY AND LEARN DIRECTLY FROM HIM!

You see, writing and teaching are a couple of my natural gifts, so God told me to *write* the stories and studies in this book to *teach* you how to get into the practice of meeting with Him every day. This book was a tool God used to get you closer to Him. He wanted you to learn how to set aside time for Him. He wanted you to get comfortable with searching the scriptures. He wanted you to see that studying His word builds your relationship with Him.

There is no doubt in my mind that if you were consistent in doing your studies every day, and if you really gave your all in the journals, challenges and activities, you are closer to Him than you've ever been. You can probably even sense His spirit speaking to you and guiding you when you're making decisions. Have you been more patient? Have you been more giving? Have you been more loving and kind toward others? Spending time with the Lord will do that!

So you definitely don't want to stop spending time with God. You're just getting started! The book's over, but you should definitely still meet with God every day and have **Quiet Time**.

WHAT IS QUIET TIME?

What Is Quiet Time?

This is a time that you set aside **every day** to meet with God. Every day that you've done studies in this book, you've been having Quiet Time.

Why Is Quiet Time Necessary?

It is unrealistic to be in a relationship with someone and think it will flourish or thrive without regular communication. It just doesn't work. How would you feel if your boyfriend was walking around school calling you his girlfriend and claiming you as his girlfriend, but never said even 2 words to you at school, never talked to you on the phone, and never texted you? Could you even call that a relationship? How can we "be together" if we don't communicate? The Holy Spirit may live in your heart, but if you're not communicating with Him, He's just there. He doesn't know you, and you don't know Him. <u>**He wants to communicate with you. He wants to know you intimately, and He wants you to know Him**</u>.

Continue Your Daily Communication With God

1. Get, or create a **journal** that is specifically for your quiet time.
2. **Turn your cell phone and television completely off!**
3. Grab your **bible**, the **book** you're reading (if you're reading one), your **journal** and a **pen**.
4. Start your quiet time with **prayer**. This is nothing more than talking to God.

5. Your prayer could be what I call a **Run Down**. This is where I write everything I feel like I need to do that day, and I ask Him to guide me. I do that because my mind is CRAZY and FULL of stuff ALL THE TIME! I want to get all that out of the way so I can have my mind clear.
6. Pray and ask God to open your understanding for your reading for the day. Then, begin reading.
7. If you're reading a book, of course, just start reading where you left off, and when the book takes you to certain scriptures, go there in your bible. Write in the margins of your book to connect your thoughts. Shoot, write all over your book—underline, circle, highlight—get what you need! Be active in your reading, just like you were in this book. It's how you get the most out of it.
8. When you're not reading a book, and it's just you and your Bible, I suggest reading a book of the Bible in succession and doing a chapter (or a section) a day. **Psalms, Proverbs, and John** are good places to start.
9. **"Talk back to Him"** after reading His word. Tell that journal what you got from the reading.
10. The last thing you want to do after you've studied your word for the day is write in your journal **HOW WHAT YOU READ APPLIES TO YOUR LIFE AND HOW YOU NEED TO WALK THAT OUT IN YOUR LIFE** (if you didn't already do that in your "Talk back to Him").
11. **End with prayer.**

WHAT IS QUIET TIME?

Let's Practice!

1. **Pray.** Tell God what you're thankful for. Thank Him for what you've learned about Him through this book. Ask Him to forgive you for anything you may have done that you didn't know was wrong. Ask Him to help you live STRONG for Him from this point on. *(There's no time constraint here. Pray as long or as short as you like—whatever you're comfortable with.)*

2. **Read Romans 10:9-13. In your own words, summarize what the Lord is saying in this passage.**

   _____

   _____

   _____

   _____

   _____

3. **Now, talk back to the Lord. What do you want to say to the Lord in response to what He just said to you in His word? How does this apply to you? How can you walk this out in your life?**

4. **End with prayer.**

Day 30
My Quiet Time

Stories THAT TEACH Girls

Pray.

Read Ephesians 6:1-3.

What is the Lord saying in this passage?

_____

_____

_____

_____

How does this apply to you?

_____

_____

_____

_____

End with prayer.

www.ingramcontent.com/pod-product-compliance
Lightning Source LLC
Chambersburg PA
CBHW080435110426
42743CB00016B/3170